Heidegger and the Environment

New Heidegger Research

Series editors:
Gregory Fried, Professor of Philosophy, Suffolk University, USA
Richard Polt, Professor of Philosophy, Xavier University, USA

The New Heidegger Research series promotes informed and critical dialogue
that breaks new philosophical ground by taking into account the full range of
Heidegger's thought, as well as the enduring questions raised by his work.

Titles in the Series:
Making Sense of Heidegger, Thomas Sheehan
Heidegger and the Environment, Casey Rentmeester
After the Greeks, Laurence Paul Hemming (forthcoming)
*The Question Concerning the Thing: On Kant's Doctrine of the
    Transcendental Principles*, Martin Heidegger, translated by Benjamin D.
    Crowe and James D. Reid (forthcoming)

Heidegger and the Environment

Casey Rentmeester

ROWMAN & LITTLEFIELD

INTERNATIONAL

London • New York

Published by Rowman & Littlefield International Ltd
Unit A, Whitacre Mews, 26-34 Stannary Street, London SE11 4AB
www.rowmaninternational.com

Rowman & Littlefield International Ltd. is an affiliate of Rowman & Littlefield
4501 Forbes Boulevard, Suite 200, Lanham, Maryland 20706, USA
With additional offices in Boulder, New York, Toronto (Canada), and Plymouth (UK)
www.rowman.com

British Library Cataloguing in Publication Data
A catalogue record for this book is available from the British Library

ISBN: HB 978-1-78348-232-0
PB 978-1-78348-233-7

Library of Congress Cataloging-in-Publication Data

Names: Rentmeester, Casey.
Title: Heidegger and the environment / Casey Rentmeester.
Description: Lanham : Rowman & Littlefield International, 2015. | Series: New
    Heidegger research | Includes bibliographical references and index.
Identifiers: LCCN 2015038718| ISBN 9781783482320 (cloth : alk. paper) | ISBN
    9781783482337 (pbk.) | ISBN 9781783482344 (electronic)
Subjects: LCSH: Heidegger, Martin, 1889–1976. | Philosophy of nature. |
    Ecology.
Classification: LCC B3279.H49 R426 2015 | DDC 193—dc23 LC record available at
http://lccn.loc.gov/2015038718

∞ ™ The paper used in this publication meets the minimum requirements of American
National Standard for Information Sciences—Permanence of Paper for Printed Library
Materials, ANSI/NISO Z39.48-1992.

Printed in the United States of America

For Amelia,
who must ever learn to dwell.

Martin Heidegger's collected works are published under the title *Gesamtausgabe* by Vittorio Klostermann (Frankfurt am Main). Throughout the book, all citations will refer to the English translations of the German texts, with a cross-listing of the pagination in the *Gesamtausgabe* abbreviated as GA. The following are the bibliographic details of the German texts to aid in cross-referencing:

GA 2: *Sein und Zeit.* Edited by Friedrich-Wilhelm von Herrmann, 1977; first edition 1927.

GA 5: *Holzwege.* Edited by Friedrich-Wilhelm von Herrmann, 1977; first edition 1950.

GA 6.1: *Nietzsche* vol. I. Edited by Brigitte Schillbach, 1996; first edition 1961.

GA 6.2: *Nietzsche* vol. II. Edited by Brigitte Schillbach, 1997; first edition 1961.

GA 7: *Vortäge und Aufsätze.* Edited by Friedrich-Wilhelm von Herrmann, 2000; first edition 1954.

GA 8: *Was heißt Denken?* Edited by Paola-Ludovika Coriando, 2002; first edition 1954.

GA 9: *Wegmarken.* Edited by Friedrich-Wilhelm von Hermmann, 1976; first edition 1967.

GA 10: *Der Satz vom Grund.* Edited by Petra Jaeger, 1997; first edition 1957.

GA 11: *Identität und Differenz.* Edited by Friedrich-Wilhelm von Herrmann, 2006.

GA 12: *Unterwegs zur Sprache.* Edited by Friedrich-Wilhelm von Herrmann, 1985; first edition 1959.

GA 13: *Aus der Erfahrung des Denkens.* Edited by Hermann Heidegger.

GA 14: *Zur Sache des Denkens.* Edited by Friedrich-Wilhelm von Herrmann, 2007; first edition 1962.

GA 15: *Seminare.* Edited by Curd Ochwadt, 1986.

GA 16: *Reden und andere Zeugnisse eines Lebens, 1910–1976.* Edited by Hermann Heidegger, 2000.

GA 18: *Grundbegriffe der aristotelischen Philosophie.* Edited by Mark Michalski, 2002.

GA 19: *Platon: Sophistes.* Edited by Ingeborg Schüßler, 1992.

GA 20: *Prolegomena zur Geschichte des Zeitbegriffs.* Edited by Petra Jaeger, 1979.

GA 24: *Die Grundprobleme der Phänomenologie*. Edited by Friedrich-Wilhelm von Herrmann, 1975.

GA 29/30: *Die Grundbegriffe der Metaphysik. Welt—Endlichkeit—Einsamkeit*. Edited by Friedrich-Wilhelm von Herrmann, 1983.

GA 31: *Vom Wesen der menschlichen Freiheit. Einleitung in die Philosophie*. Edited by Harmut Tietjen, 1982.

GA 39: *Hölderlins Hymnen "Germanien" und "Der Rhein."* Edited by Susanne Ziegler, 1980.

GA 40: *Einführung in die Metaphysik*. Edited by Petra Jaeger, 1983; first edition 1953.

GA 41: *Die Frage nach dem Ding. Zu Kants Lehre von den transzendentalen Grundsätzen*. Edited by Petra Jaeger, 1984; first edition 1962.

GA 47: *Nietzsches Lehre vom Willen zur Macht als Erkenntnis*. Edited by Eberhard Hanser, 1989; first edition 1961.

GA 54: *Parmenides*. Edited by Manfred S. Frings, 1982.

GA 56/57: *Zur Bestimmung der Philosophie*. Edited by Bernd Heimbüchel, 1987.

GA 58: *Grundprobleme der Phänomenologie*. Edited by Hans-Helmut Gander, 1992.

GA 60: *Phänomenologie der Anschauung und des Ausdrucks*. Edited by Claudius Strube, 1993.

GA 63: *Ontologie. Hermeneutik der Faktizität*. Edited by Käte Bröcker-Oltmanns, 1988.

GA 65: *Beiträge zur Philosophie (Vom Ereignis)*. Edited by Friedrich-Wilhelm von Herrmann, 1989.

GA 66: *Besinnung*. Edited by Friedrich-Wilhelm von Herrmann, 1997.

GA 77: *Feldwege-Gespräche 1944/45*. Edited by Ingrid Schüßler, 2007; first edition 1995.

GA 79: *Bremer und Freiburger Vorträge*. Edited by Petra Jaeger, 1994.

GA 94: *Überlegungen II–VI (Scharze Hefte 1931–1938)*. Edited by Peter Trawny, 2014.

GA 95: *Überlegungen VII–XI (Scharze Hefte 1938–1939)*. Edited by Peter Trawny, 2014.

GA 96: *Überlegungen XII–XV (Scharze Hefte 1939–1941)*. Edited by Peter Trawny, 2014.

Contents

Preface

Modern environmentalism has had a short but important history. Many point to Rachel Carson's *Silent Spring* of 1962 as its inception.[1] Here, Carson, a marine biologist, demonstrated the harms of pesticides and herbicides to wildlife, habitats, and humans. In many ways, her work led to the banning of the pesticide dichlorodiphenyltrichloroethane—more commonly known as DDT—by the U.S. government a decade later. By the 1970s, environmentalism began to be integrated into academia, and the initial movement—sparked in part by Peter Singer's *Animal Liberation* of 1975—dealt mostly with the inclusion of environmentalism into the field of ethics.[2] Singer, an Oxford-trained ethicist who had already made a splash in the academic community with his 1972 article "Famine, Affluence and Morality," gave the animal rights movement legitimacy in the field of philosophy.[3] He approaches the issue of animal rights from a utilitarian perspective, showing that anyone who cares about minimizing pain and maximizing pleasure must take the pains and pleasures of nonhuman animals into moral consideration since pain is bad, whether experienced by a human being or a nonhuman animal.[4] By 1979, we saw the introduction of the first peer-reviewed academic journal in environmental philosophy in the United States—the still existent *Environmental Ethics*—and we now have a good number of academic journals devoted to environmentalism in general and environmental ethics in particular. In fact, it is safe to say that the field of environmental philosophy is now a full-fledged, respected subdiscipline of philosophy, as many colleges and universities offer classes in this subject.

Most of the articles in these journals and most of the classes taught still approach environmentalism from an ethical perspective, using some moral theory (e.g., utilitarianism, deontology, etc.) and applying it to a particular environmental issue. This is not surprising, given that the initial academic work on this topic—the work of Peter Singer—utilized this approach. If we want to put this in Kuhnian terms, we could say that Singer determined what environmental philosophy should look like, thereby establishing a paradigm of what it means to do environmental philosophy.[5] Though there are some outliers to this basic approach, most of the work done in this field still works from the basis of this paradigm, and environmental philosophy has thus been largely considered to be discipline of *applied* ethics. In other words, environmental philosophers typically approach an environmental issue from a specific ethical background and attempt to expand our realm of moral consideration to include a new set of natural entities, whether it be nonhuman animals, living things, or even nature itself by applying ethical principles to such entities. Singer's *Animal Liberation* extends the realm of moral consideration to nonhuman animals by showing that nonhuman animals are sentient. The basic idea here is that we take other human beings into moral consideration because they have "the capacity to suffer and/or experience enjoyment"[6] and, since animals are sentient as well, we must also take them into moral consideration if we are to be consistent.

The other champion of the animal rights movement, Tom Regan, takes a similar approach. Coming from a deontological perspective, Regan argues that what makes something morally considerable is the fact that it is a subject-of-a-life, that is, an individual who has

> beliefs and desires; perception, memory, and a sense of the future, including [one's] own future; an emotional life together with feelings of pleasure and pain; preference- and welfare-interests; the ability to initiate action in the pursuit of [one's] own desires and goals; a psychophysical identity over time; and an individual welfare in the sense that [one's] experiential life fares well or ill for [one], logically independently of [one's] utility for others and logically independently of [one's] being the object of anyone else's interests.[7]

The reasoning behind Regan's case for animal rights is similar to Singer's in that he establishes what one must have in order to receive moral consideration and then shows that this characteristic is something that we share with other animals. Though they disagree as to the criteria meriting moral consideration, the idea of extending the realm of entities that deserve moral consideration still holds. We can call such approaches *zoocentric* in that they attempt to extend moral consideration to other entities in the animal kingdom.

Similar approaches can be found if we look beyond the animal rights movement and look to *biocentric* ethics. The objective here is to expand the realm of moral consideration to include not just animals but all living things. Perhaps the most famous recent proponent of a biocentric ethic is Paul Taylor. In his 1986 work, *Respect for Nature*, Taylor argues that each teleological center of life, which he defines as a "unified, coherently ordered system of goal-oriented activities that has a constant tendency to protect and maintain the organism's existence,"[8] has inherent worth that must be respected. The logic here mimics what we find in Singer and Regan. The goal is to determine what characteristic makes humans worthy of moral consideration—in this case, being a teleological center of life—and then show that this characteristic is something we share with other living beings, making them worthy of respect as well.

While mainstream environmental philosophy still works within this realm of applied ethics, recent developments in the field have opened up the discipline beyond this narrow focus. With the movements of deep ecology and ecofeminism in the 1970s and 1980s, philosophers began to question the legitimacy of framing environmental issues in the traditional ethical formats. Rather than approaching issues from utilitarian or deontological perspectives, such approaches question the legitimacy of pigeonholing environmental philosophy as a discipline of applied ethics in the first place. Deep ecologists, whose work was sparked initially by the work of Arne Naess, question the assumptions of our Western worldview and emphasize the importance of philosophical concepts from Eastern philosophies and minority traditions.[9] Ecofeminists, influenced by feminist philosophers who critique mainstream Western philosophy, argue that there is a link between the domination of women and the domination of nature and criticize the logic of both.[10] In many ways, deep ecology and ecofeminism opened up environmental philosophy beyond the narrow straits of applied ethics into more inclusive realms. Instead of taking a nonhuman entity and giving it moral consideration due to a novel application of ethical theory, deep ecologists and ecofeminists provide a new model built upon (1) a critique of traditional or mainstream philosophy and (2) a view built upon the scaffolding of a minority tradition.

Such approaches in environmental philosophy have provided novel avenues from which to approach environmentalism. One of the more recent developments stemming from such an approach is eco-phenomenology, which Iain Thomson explains as follows: "Eco-phenomenology's guiding idea, put simply, is that uprooting and replacing some of our deeply-entrenched but environmentally-destructive ethical and metaphysical presuppositions can help us heal the earth, combating environmental devastation at its conceptual roots, as it were."[11]

Charles Brown and Ted Toadvine, two advocates of the eco-phenomenology movement, point out that eco-phenomenology is not simply a critical enterprise since it offers alternative approaches to environmentalism as well. They state, "For environmental philosophers, phenomenology suggests alternatives to many of the ingrained tendencies that limit our inherited perspectives."[12] Edmund Husserl established phenomenology as a philosophical movement in the first half of the twentieth century. One of the most famous phenomenologists is Husserl's student, Martin Heidegger (1889–1976), who is widely regarded as one of the greatest thinkers of the twentieth century. Since one of Heidegger's main goals was to critique the reified traditions of Western philosophy and open up new ways of understanding reality, he is a fitting candidate for an eco-phenomenological approach to environmentalism. In this book, I use Heidegger's phenomenological critique of Western metaphysics to show which concepts provide the theoretical sanctions for environmental destruction. I then use elements of Heidegger's later thought to provide the scaffolding for an environmental ethic, which I juxtapose with philosophical Daoism to show what a nonmetaphysical ethics may look like. Heidegger's philosophy provides us with a solid basis from which to approach the environment from a conceptual perspective, which I aim to build upon in order to provide a new path in environmental philosophy.

HEIDEGGER AND ENVIRONMENTALISM

Before embarking upon a Heideggerian version of environmentalism, we should chronicle the relationship Heidegger has had with the environmental tradition. Clare Palmer rightly notes that "serious philosophical reflection about ethical issues raised by human action in the nonhuman natural world commenced in the early 1970s."[13] The first Earth Day of 1970 raised global awareness of the need for environmental protection, which eventually generated discussion among intellectuals as to which aspects of our traditions could provide a philosophical basis for this movement. Georg Seidel's brief article from 1971 directly poses the question as to whether Heidegger could be a viable candidate. Focusing on what he calls Heidegger's "authentic knowing," which entails allowing beings to come to light on their own terms, Seidel argues that Heidegger is "a possible philosopher for the ecologists."[14] Hwa Yol Jung and Petee Jung take up this project of utilizing Heidegger's philosophy to build an environmental ethic in their article a few years later, although their respective backgrounds in political science and mathematics lead to a peculiar reading of Heidegger's philosophy. For instance, they translate *Ereignis*—one of Heidegger's most important yet elusive concepts—as "social principle" and equate it with the "synchronicity" that is found in the Chinese classic, the *I Ching* (易經).[15] Most Heidegger scholars would surely disagree with this translation of *Ereignis*, which is typically translated as "appropriation" and doesn't have the socio-political connotation that Jung and Jung read into it. Also, while Jung and Jung show insight by exploring some conceptual similarities between Heidegger's thought and Chinese philosophy—a link that has been corroborated by later interpreters and one I will explore in my own way in chapter 5—their way of equating *Ereignis* with synchronicity is a stretch. Nevertheless, their claim that Heidegger's concept of *Gelassenheit*, which I will translate as "letting beings be," parallels the Daoist practice of *wúwéi* (無為) is insightful.[16]

Michael Zimmerman takes up the task of showing Heidegger to be a useful philosopher for environmentalists in a series of articles in the 1980s, and he publishes the first book-length, rigorous analysis of Heidegger's thought and environmentalism in 1990.[17] *Heidegger's Confrontation with Modernity* is an impressive scholarly work that chronicles the social, political, and intellectual influences of Heidegger's thought *en route* to a Heideggerian response to what Zimmerman rightly calls "technological nihilism," that is, a world devoid of meaning and devoted solely to maximizing efficiency in the realms of industry and technology. In tracing the "productionist metaphysics" that begins with Plato in ancient Greece and ends in Friedrich Nietzsche's concept of the will to power in which a thing's value is understood as "enhancing the Will to Will,"[18] Zimmerman demonstrates how Heidegger's thought provides the opportunity of opening up a more authentic relationship to things: "If we are to treat things appropriately . . . we must at least become attuned and receptive to those things as much as we can within the limits of the conceptual grid which helps to determine how things can show themselves. For Heidegger, such a receptive approach to things was central to all authentic producing, understood as the disclosive act of letting something be."[19] Zimmerman points to ancient Greek artisans as persons who engaged in authentic production. With the onset of technological nihilism partially triggered by the Industrial Revolution, we simply no longer engage in such production but rather myopically produce things in ways that maximize efficiency. In his quest for a response to technological nihilism, Zimmerman explicitly provides aspects of Heidegger's thought to support the claim that he is "a major deep ecological theorist" in the book, thereby putting Heidegger on the environmental map.[20]

In fact, Zimmerman's work opens up an entire Heideggerian avenue for philosophers to traverse as they attempt to determine guiding intellectual voices in the burgeoning environmental movement. In 1992, Charles Taylor rightly points to the importance of language in this attempt, noting "our status as language beings can be thought to lay us open to ecologically relevant demands,"[21] a claim I will corroborate in chapter 1. Ladelle McWhorter edits an entire volume devoted to showing the link between Heidegger and environmentalism in the same year, titled *Heidegger and the Earth*.[22] Using various creative techniques, from emphasizing Heidegger's concept of guilt in *Being and Time* to interpretations of various poetic verses, the authors provide unique perspectives on the Heidegger–environmentalism connection. As Tara Kennedy notes, however, "a worry regarding the practical effectiveness of a Heideggerian approach to the environment remains."[23] This worry is exacerbated by the fact that Zimmerman himself rethinks the Heidegger–environmentalism connection the following year due to Heidegger's engagement with National Socialism. While in 1990 Zimmerman argues that this engagement "was an attempt to realize in the political domain his own conviction about the need to reunite the artistic and productive realms,"[24] by 1993 he considered Heidegger's Nazism to be incompatible with the environmental movement that he once considered Heidegger to be a forerunner for: that of deep ecology.[25] Given that Zimmerman was largely responsible for putting Heidegger on the environmental map, his concerns regarding the possibility of a Heideggerian version of environmentalism could have provided the death blow to further research into this connection.

Undeterred, Bruce Foltz revives Heidegger's philosophy as a potential intellectual basis for environmentalism in 1995 with his excellent book, *Inhabiting the Earth*, in which he argues that "the rift between ourselves and the natural environment that has resulted in the environmental crisis . . . cannot be healed by additional scientific research or more efficient technological regulation, but only through a poetic reestablishing of those world-regions within whose dimensions we can dwell and be at home."[26] Foltz takes Heidegger's interest in the German poet Friedrich Hölderlin as the key to what poetically dwelling entails, and equates ethics with understanding what it means "to dwell within the midst of beings as a whole."[27] *Inhabiting the Earth* is a paragon of scholarship, and is especially helpful in diagnosing problems with the technological domination of nature. There are, however, some questions that arise when considering the narrative that Foltz sets up. Foltz explicitly aims to restore the rift between human beings and the natural environment. Zimmerman has pointed out, however, that "[Heidegger's] anti-naturalistic stance led some deep ecologists to suspect that despite many indications that his thought had a green dimension, Heidegger adhered to the humanity–nature dualism and anthropocentrism that have helped generate the ecological crisis."[28] In fact, Zimmerman himself has argued that Heidegger "believed that humankind is discontinuous with nature,"[29] and therefore could never mend the rift between humans and nature. Moreover, Foltz's attempt to interpret ethics as understanding how to dwell may fall prey to Zimmerman's claim that Heidegger's explicit denial of espousing an ethics in the normative sense may mean "the central core of his thought provides inadequate guidance for environmental philosophy."[30] I will attempt to defend Foltz's basic thesis that Heidegger can be used as an intellectual grounding for an environmental philosophy, but will focus in on different aspects of Heidegger's thought than the poetic aspects that Foltz relies heavily upon.

Recently, as the field of eco-phenomenology has gained traction, philosophers have explicitly utilized phenomenological methods to engage the relationship between Heidegger and environmentalism. Neil Evernden's *The Natural Alien* from 1985 can be seen as a forerunner to the eco-phenomenology movement. Here, Evernden uses Heidegger in his project of placing environmental philosophy on a new path. He states, "We cannot correct our path by adding qualifications to existing assumptions,"[31] and while he only spends about a chapter on Heidegger's thought, he notes that Heidegger's quest to overcome metaphysics is in line with saving the earth.[32] Despite the brevity of Evernden's engagement with Heidegger and environmentalism, he provides a basis from which to work. The edited volume *Eco-Phenomenology*, from 2003, provides the clearest sampling of what the eco-phenomenological movement entails. In it, Monika Langer provides a basic outline as to what a Heideggerian eco-phenomenology would look like in linking Heidegger's concepts of meditative thinking with letting beings be and care.[33] While she doesn't go into detail, she does echo Charles Taylor by noting that a first step towards a Heideggerian eco-phenomenology lies in "recognizing that thought and language are internally related, and that they involve an entire way of living."[34] At the same time, she claims that Heidegger's philosophy may be too anthropocentric for environmentalists to take up since he sets humans apart from other beings. I will argue below that Heidegger's human exceptionalism is actually an asset to his philosophy.

Following the seeds sown by Langer, Kevin Michael Deluca presents Heidegger as a breath of fresh air for environmentalists in his 2005 article, "Thinking with Heidegger." While Deluca explicitly rejects Heidegger's ontology, he notes that Heidegger's critique of machination may offer a new perspective in environmental philosophical circles to counteract the dominant trend of Cartesianism wherein the human subject is regarded as controller or manager of nature.[35] I will flesh out Heidegger's critique of Cartesianism and machination in chapter 3. A few years later, Ruth Irwin takes up the task of using Heidegger's thought to engage the issue of climate change in her book, *Heidegger, Politics and Climate Change*. Here, Irwin argues that Heidegger's "other 'beginning' is recognition of the finitude of civilization itself and of human life as-a-whole on the planet."[36] Climate change should get human beings to reflect on the nihilism involved in the way of life of most humans in the contemporary age and "initiate a paradigm shift that integrates humanity with nature."[37] While I think Irwin's way of mapping Heidegger's thought onto the climate crisis itself is problematic and that her aim to integrate humanity with nature is not true to Heidegger's task, her attempt of using Heidegger's thought to dwell on an appropriate response to the climate crisis is novel and insightful. Irwin's 2010 article, "Reflections on Modern Climate Change and Finitude," is another attempt to reflect on climate change from a Heideggerian lens. Here, she views economics and consumerism from the lens of Heideggerian enframing and urges us to move beyond our myopic understanding of reality. Rightly noting that "climate change is a crisis of mastery over nature,"[38] she again argues that a reflection on the finitude of civilization can get us to move beyond mastery and initiate a more appropriate relationship with nature.

Bryan Bannon takes up this narrative of moving beyond mastery in his 2014 book, *From Mastery to Mystery*. Using eco-phenomenology as his background, Bannon notes several aspects that we can learn from Heidegger in our attempt to develop an eco-phenomenology:

1. An attempt to be open to understandings of the natural environment that are not ensconced in narratives of mastery that stem from Cartesianism.
2. An attempt to move beyond the Western metaphysical tradition.
3. An appreciation of the relationality of all beings.[39]

I will try to corroborate and expand upon Bannon's claims regarding the fruitful aspects of Heidegger's philosophy for environmentalism even though Bannon ultimately argues that Maurice Merleau-Ponty is the more appropriate eco-phenomenological thinker due to Heidegger's way of privileging the status of human beings in nature.[40]

My aim will be to build upon the foundations of those who have written on the Heidegger–environmentalism connection before while at the same time updating this specific connection to the current environmental crisis, which is signaled by anthropogenic climate change. Put simply, I hope to show that the present predicament merits a new voice in environmentalism. While traditional ethical approaches to environmentalism can prove fruitful, Heidegger's thought is unique in that he provides an ontological analysis of the metaphysical tradition that has allowed for the environmental crisis to occur. For Heidegger, "The question concerning our basic relations to nature, our knowledge of nature as such, our rule over nature, is not a question of natural science, but this question is itself in question in *the* question of whether and how we are still addressed by what is as such within the whole."[41] In other words, our relationship to nature is informed by our understanding of what it means for anything to *be* at all. The fundamental question I aim to pose from a Heideggerian lens—"What is our proper relationship to the natural world?"—elicits a deeper question into what ultimately matters for contemporary human beings. If we are to situate this in the history of modern environmentalism, this is precisely the sort of questioning demanded by deep ecologists; in fact, the first deep ecologists—Arne Naess, Bill Devall, and George Sessions—all considered Heidegger to be a source of inspiration for their movement.[42] However, as I argue in chapter 1, there are significant ways in which Heidegger's thought differs from the tenets of deep ecology. I therefore see Heidegger's contribution to environmentalism to be properly situated in the realm of eco-phenomenology.

INITIAL OBSTACLES

Attempts to construe Heidegger as a potential asset to environmentalism have sometimes been met with skepticism or even outright denial. The three overarching obstacles with using Heidegger as a novel source in environmentalism are as follows: (1) the concern of anthropocentrism; (2) Heidegger's relationship with Nazism; and (3) Heidegger's rejection of normative ethics. I shall deal briefly with these concerns before commencing the attempt to build a Heideggerian environmental ethic.

Perhaps the most commonly noted concern regarding Heidegger and environmentalism is his purported anthropocentrism. The term "anthropocentrism" became a popular label in the 1980s for theories that put humankind at the center of the universe.[43] Historically, much of the field of environmental philosophy has been dominated by the debate as to whether our ethical approaches should be anthropocentric or antianthropocentric. Anthropocentrism, roughly stated, is centered around the claim that human beings are the most important entities on the planet and that any ethical theories should recognize and respect humans as such. Those who argue for anthropocentric approaches to environmentalism argue that any environmental policies should be cognizant of this fact, rather than act as if humans were just one "natural" species among many. The best explicitly stated example of this position I have come across is from Polish philosopher Henryk Skolimowski, who states, "All claims made on behalf of the biotic community are made by human beings; they are filtered by human sensitivities and by human compassion; they are based on our human sense of justice, on our human recognition of how things are and how they ought to be; they are pervaded with human values—all these claims are therefore deeply and profoundly embedded in our anthropocentrism, whether we care to recognize this or not."[44]

Anthropocentricists argue that all values are necessarily human values and are therefore human-centered; thus, any environmental ethic must be anthropocentric. Antianthropocentric approaches, on the other hand, deny this privileged status to human beings. Perhaps the most notable quote expressing the antianthropocentric attitude comes from Aldo Leopold, who famously argues for a change in "the role of *Homo sapiens* from conqueror of the land-community to plain member and citizen of it."[45] Instead of viewing the natural world from our human perspective, which is necessarily biased in our favor, Leopold encourages us to "think like a mountain," since "only the mountain has lived long enough to listen objectively to the howl of a wolf."[46] This antianthropocentric stance can be seen in the "inhumanist" poetry of Robinson Jeffers, whom Devall and Sessions cite explicitly as a contributor to the deep ecology movement.[47]

In his 1938 work, "The Age of the World Picture," Heidegger argues against "that philosophical interpretation of man which explains and evaluates whatever is, in its entirety, from the standpoint of man and in relation to man."[48] Therefore, he wouldn't simply agree with a version of anthropocentrism akin to Skolimowski's. At the same time, however, Heidegger would certainly not agree with Leopold that humans are "plain members and citizens" of the earth since he repeatedly stresses the uniqueness of the human being. On the one hand, Heidegger does admit that "man obviously is a being. As such he belongs to the totality of being—just like the stone, the tree, or the eagle. To 'belong' here still means to be in the order of being."[49] On the other hand, Heidegger explicitly says that humans are separated from all other living creatures "by an abyss."[50] Zimmerman points out that this shows that Heidegger "believed that humankind is discontinuous with nature as understood by physics, chemistry, biology, and psychology."[51] Zimmerman is right to note that one aspect of the human is discontinuous with other entities in the natural world; at the same time, Heidegger recognizes continuity with human beings and other natural beings. In order to understand this, we have to clearly delineate the human being in its scientific categorization, the human being in general, and the human being in its essence [*Wesen*].[52] Scientifically, the human being is properly classified as the species *Homo sapiens* and can be analyzed as such. Physical, chemical, and biological analyses of human beings gain knowledge of the human in this regard. Since Heidegger is not a scientist, interpreting the human being from this perspective would be inappropriate.[53] The human being in general is the ἄνθρωπος [*anthropos*], which the ancient Greeks would juxtapose with the gods. Heidegger uses the word *Mensch* or *Dasein* in a way similar to how the Greeks would use ἄνθρωπος.[54] He also speaks of the *Da-sein* [being-there] or *Existenz* [existence] of the human being, which is the essence of the human.[55] It is this aspect of the human being that distinguishes the human from the rest of the natural world. After showing how we are on a continuum with all other beings, he states, "But man's distinctive feature lies in this, that he, as the being who thinks, is open to being, face to face with being; thus man remains referred to being and answers to it."[56] Here, Heidegger is saying that though humans are similar to all other beings in certain respects, our distinctive feature lies in our ability to respond to the ways in which entities unfold in significant ways. It is this aspect of the human being that is "abysmally" different from all other living beings.

While Heidegger admits that humans are like animals in one aspect of our being—our evolutionary or scientific aspect—he argues that our essence is fundamentally different from animals: "Because plants and animals are lodged in their respective environments but are never placed freely into the clearing of being which alone is 'world,' they lack language."[57] As far as we know, only human beings have worlds, that is, only human beings are open to complex relations of significance. This is important insofar as it allows us to *change* our world in accordance with our interests. I will argue in chapter 1 that it is this openness to being that allows the human being to be such an environmentally destructive entity. At the same time, however, our essence allows us to take a step back and reflect on a more appropriate relationship with nature, which is precisely where a Heideggerian environmental ethic provides a unique perspective in that it respects the uniqueness of the human being without sanctioning reckless exploitation of the environment.

The second potential obstacle to espousing a Heideggerian environmental ethic lies in Heidegger's relationship with Nazism. Thousands upon thousands of pages have been written on the connection between Heidegger and Nazism, and without going into too much detail, it is clear that Heidegger was energetically committed to National Socialism in the early 1930s, was anti-Semitic in some regard, and believed at one time that Adolf Hitler was the proper leader to unite the German people. This has led to varying levels of reactions from Heidegger scholars. On one end of the spectrum, Emmanuel Faye has argued that "Nazism . . . inspired [Heidegger's] works in their entirety"[58] and, therefore, Heidegger's works should be no longer be categorized as philosophy but rather as Nazism or Hitlerism.[59] At the other end of the spectrum, Jürgen Habermas, who called for a public explanation of Heidegger's relationship with Nazism in 1953[60] but never received one, has argued "illumination of the political conduct of Martin Heidegger cannot and should not serve the purpose of a global depreciation of his thought"[61] since we should detach the politics of the person from the philosophy. It is clear that Heidegger did occasionally use his philosophy to support anti-Semitic and Nazi ideologies, especially in the so-called *Schwarze Hefte* [Black Notebooks] in which he links Jewry with "worldlessness"[62] and "empty rationality."[63] Given this, it is inappropriate to make a simple distinction between Heidegger's philosophy and his politics. However, this does not mean that we should disregard Heidegger as a first-rate thinker. As Richard Polt and Gregory Fried claim, it is our responsibility as interpreters to "disentangle the truer or more promising aspects of his philosophy from the pernicious ones."[64]

Having said this, it is important to recall that Zimmerman has expressed worries regarding Heidegger's Nazism and its link to environmentalism. In *Contesting the Earth's Future*, he frankly asserts that his "increased understanding of the link between Heidegger's thought and has politics . . . [has led him] to be more skeptical of grand proposals for revolutionary change, including those based on fears of an ecological crisis."[65] The biggest worry in this regard is that Heidegger's thought could prescribe some version of Eco-fascism, a political program that uses Fascist methods to remedy environmental degradation.[66] An example of an Ecofascist approach would be to kill off some human beings if they were to exceed their carrying capacity in a given geographical region. Peter Staudenmaier has argued that Heidegger "helped bridge fascism and environmentalism,"[67] while Thomas Rohkrämer has stated that "it was only a consequence of his disappointment with Nazism that the question of technology and environmentalism became central to Heidegger's thinking."[68] The claim that Heidegger helped bridge fascism and environmentalism assumes that Heidegger was influential in either sphere, when in fact he was not in either. While Heidegger did have dreams of being the leading philosophical voice of the Nazi Party, he had very little actual influence. Although he served as rector for the University of Freiburg for one year, the Nazi Party regarded him as "completely expendable" in 1944.[69] In regard to environmentalism, this movement didn't gain major traction until after Heidegger's death and, therefore, Heidegger certainly wouldn't have identified himself as an environmentalist. Moreover, given that environmental philosophy has largely been a discipline of applied ethics, Heidegger has not yet been highly influential in environmental circles. Nevertheless, the scaffolding of an environmental ethic that I attempt to build from his thought may pose a worry of Ecofascist undertones for some.

In regard to Heidegger's occasional inherent linkage of philosophy and political ideology, it is important to point out that while Heidegger was enthralled with Hitler in the early 1930s, he became disillusioned with Hitler later in the decade. In the early 1930s, Heidegger lists four types of people that are able to set up a world authentically: creators, poets, thinkers, and statesmen.[70] Following Fried, we can say that Heidegger believed statesmen to be able to establish "the social and political order of a regime by which human beings take their measure and find their bearing."[71] As Zimmerman notes, "There is no reason to doubt the sincerity of [Heidegger's] belief in 1933–34 that Hitler was the statesman required to carry out Heidegger's spiritual vision."[72] The Nazis did have somewhat of a "green" platform in that they created nature preserves and emphasized being close to nature.[73] If we couple this with the horrific practices of genocide during the Holocaust, one may be able to concoct an argument that the Nazis could have implemented an Ecofascist regime wherein human beings are killed in the name of the health of the environment. Since Heidegger was a National Socialist and temporarily used his philosophy to bolster Nazi ideology, one may worry that a Heideggerian version of environmentalism may fall prey to Ecofacism. Towards the end of the decade, however, when he first provides detailed analyses of nature and technology, Heidegger no longer lists statesmen in the same category as creators, poets, and thinkers. Indeed, Heidegger explicitly critiques Hitler in his private notes from the late 1930s, now published as *Mindfulness* [*Besinnung*].[74] Following the advice of Polt and Fried, Heidegger's brief linkage of philosophy and political ideology will be one of the elements I leave to the wayside. After all, the Heideggerian version of environmentalism I will argue for is not a top-down endeavor wherein a political leader calls the shots that citizens must abide by; it is rather a bottom-up endeavor wherein individual human beings may be open to environmentally pressing demands and dwell among things in environmentally sustainable ways. Therefore, despite Heidegger's lamentable relationship with National Socialism, there is no worry of Ecofascism when it comes to a Heideggerian environmental philosophy.

The third obstacle to a Heideggerian environmental ethic is that Heidegger himself eschewed ethics in the normative sense of the term throughout almost his entire oeuvre. From his earliest lectures of 1919, where he says that "Being and ought, i.e., Being and value, as two worlds fundamentally different in their basic structures, are separated from one another by a chasm,"[75] to his last published works, where he explicitly distances his thought from ethics, Heidegger repeatedly emphasizes that he is espousing an ontology, that is, a study of being, rather than an ethics.[76] Heidegger believes that ethics in the sense of valuing certain types of actions over others (as one finds in, say, utilitarianism or Kantian deontology) is dependent on a subject–object ontology since it implies that a subject values certain entities over others in accordance with some preset valuation system.[77] From a Heideggerian perspective, it is precisely this sort of ontological orientation that leads to ecological destruction, as I argue in chapter 2. Therefore, a Heideggerian environmental ethic would certainly not prescribe a valuation system like a typical normative ethical theory would as in, say, a zoocentric or biocentric environmentalist approach.

The lack of a valuation system does not, however, preclude Heidegger from being an asset to environmentalism. One of the early voices of environmentalism, Arne Naess, once argued that a proper environmentalism must "*move from ontology to ethics.*"[78] For Naess, this means that one cannot have an appropriate relationship with the world ethically unless one has an appropriate understanding of what the world *is*. Heidegger's analysis of the Western metaphysical tradition and the ethical theories that have evolved from it give us some sense as to how our ontology has evolved into a specific ethical orientation in the Western world, and his later philosophy provides an ontological scaffolding from which I will attempt to build an environmental ethic upon. Indeed, I will argue in chapter 5 that Heidegger's ontology is inextricably linked to ethics. Environmental philosophy from a Heideggerian perspective will surely not be a version of applied ethics since Heidegger does not explicitly provide a normative ethical theory. Nevertheless, his thought does provide us with a pathway from which to blaze a new trail in environmentalism. This trail begins with—as Foltz notes—the critical task of an analysis of the metaphysical tradition that has undergirded our contemporary understanding of nature and the positive task of becoming "ontological midwives" who are responsive to the ways in which entities manifest themselves on their own terms.[79] I will argue that this *responsiveness* must be coupled with a *responsibility* to care for the natural world. Heidegger's thought can, in other words, provide us with the platform from which to build an environmental ethic upon, though his thought is not necessarily "environmentalistic" in and of itself. Interestingly, one finds a similar dynamic in versions of applied ethics. Immanuel Kant, for instance, was no environmentalist: he divided the world into things and persons, and only persons, that is, rational beings, merited moral consideration. Nonrational living beings such as nonhuman animals and plants fall under the category of "things" from a strictly Kantian perspective.[80] Yet Kant's philosophy has inspired many versions of environmental ethics, from the aforementioned animal rights ethics of Regan to current movements of climate ethics.[81] I argue that although Heidegger is no environmentalist and no ethicist, his thought provides the basis from which to build an environmental ethic. In many ways, the Heideggerian version of an environmental ethic echoes what may be found in philosophical Daoism, which is one of the first known environmentally conscious traditions. Though neither Heidegger's philosophy nor Daoism is properly understood as ethical in the normative sense, both offer an environmentally sustainable image of the human–nature relationship, as I argue in chapter 5.

NOTES

1. Rachel Carson, *Silent Spring* (Boston: Houghton Mifflin, 1962).

2. Peter Singer, *Animal Liberation* (New York: HarperCollins, 2002).

3. Peter Singer, "Famine, Affluence, and Morality." *Philosophy and Public Affairs* 1, no. 1 (1972): 229–243.

4. Cf. Singer, *Animal Liberation*, 20–21.

5. Thomas Kuhn, *The Structure of Scientific Revolutions* (Chicago: University of Chicago Press, 1962).

6. Singer, *Animal Liberation*, 8–9.

7. Tom Regan, *The Case for Animal Rights* (Berkeley and Los Angeles: University of California Press, 2004), 243.

8. Paul W. Taylor, *Respect for Nature: A Theory of Environmental Ethics* (Princeton: Princeton University Press, 2011), 122.

9. Arne Naess, "The Shallow and the Deep, Long-Range Ecology Movement: A Summary," *Inquiry* 16, no. 1 (1973): 95–100.

10. For an impressive summary of ecofeminism through 2001, see Victoria Davion, "Ecofeminism," in *A Companion to Environmental Philosophy*, ed. Dale Jamieson (Malden, Mass.: Blackwell Publishing, 2001), 233–247.

11. Iain Thomson, "Ontology and Ethics at the Intersection of Phenomenology and Environmental Philosophy," *Inquiry* 47, no. 4 (2004): 381.

12. Charles S. Brown and Ted Toadvine, "Eco-Phenomenology: An Introduction," in *Eco-Phenomenology: Back to the Earth Itself*, ed. Charles S. Brown and Ted Toadvine (Albany: State University of New York Press, 2003), xii.

13. Clare Palmer, "A Bibliographic Essay on Environmental Ethics," *Studies in Christian Ethics* 7, no. 1 (1994): 69.

14. Georg Seidel, "Heidegger: Philosopher for Ecologists?" *Man and World* 4, no. 1 (1971): 97. For Seidel, the word "ecologist" should be understood loosely as those interested in environmental protection and not in the more narrow subscientific discipline with which we associate it today.

15. Hwa Yol Jung and Petee Jung, "To Save the Earth," *Philosophy Today* 19, no. 2 (1975): 110. I will offer a detailed analysis of *Ereignis* in chapter 4.

16. Jung and Jung, "To Save the Earth," 114.

17. Cf. Michael E. Zimmerman, "Toward a Heideggerean *Ethos* for Radical Environmentalism," *Environmental Ethics* 5, no. 2 (1983): 99–131 and his "Implications of Heidegger's Thought for Deep Ecology," *The Modern Schoolman* 64, no. 1 (1986): 19–43.

18. Michael E. Zimmerman, *Heidegger's Confrontation with Modernity: Technology, Politics, Art* (Bloomington and Indianapolis: Indiana University Press, 1990), 173.

19. Zimmerman, *Heidegger's Confrontation with Modernity*, 228.

20. Zimmerman, *Heidegger's Confrontation with Modernity*, 243. Zimmerman does, however, caution those who are quick to adopt Heidegger as a deep ecological thinker insofar as the following aspects of Heidegger's thought that are dissonant with deep ecology: his "(1) residual anthropocentrism, (2) the reactionary dimension to his critique of industrialism and modernity, and (3) his antipathy toward science."

21. Charles Taylor, "Heidegger, Language, and Ecology," in *Heidegger: A Critical Reader*, ed. Hubert L. Dreyfus and Harrison Hall (Cambridge, Mass.: Blackwell, 1992), 247.

22. *Heidegger and the Earth: Essays in Environmental Philosophy*, ed. Ladelle McWhorter (Kirksville, Mo.: Thomas Jefferson University Press, 1992). A more recent, expanded version of this volume, which is edited by Ladelle McWhorter and Gail Stenstad, came out in 2009 from the University of Toronto Press.

23. Tara Kennedy, "Book Review: *Heidegger and the Earth: Essays in Environmental Philosophy*," *Environmental Ethics* 33, no. 1 (2011): 95.

24. Zimmerman, *Heidegger's Confrontation with Modernity*, 231.

25. Michael E. Zimmerman, "Rethinking the Heidegger-Deep Ecology Relationship," *Environmental Ethics* 15, no. 3 (1993): 195–224.

26. Bruce V. Foltz, *Inhabiting the Earth: Heidegger, Environmental Ethics, and the Metaphysics of Nature* (New York: Humanity Books, 1995), 158–159.

27. Foltz, *Inhabiting the Earth*, 168.

28. Michael E. Zimmerman, "Martin Heidegger: Anti-Naturalistic Critic of Technological Modernity," in *Minding Nature: The Philosophers of Ecology*, ed. David Macauley (New York: Guilford, 1995), 60.

29. Michael E. Zimmerman, "Heidegger's Phenomenology and Contemporary Environmentalism," in *Eco-Phenomenology: Back to the Earth Itself*, ed. Charles S. Brown and Ted Toadvine (Albany: State University of New York Press, 2003), 73–74.

30. Michael E. Zimmerman, "Heidegger's Phenomenology and Contemporary Environmentalism," 95. I will deal with this issue below.

31. Neil Evernden, *The Natural Alien: Humankind and Environment*, second edition (Toronto: University of Toronto Press, 1999), 60.

32. Cf. Evernden, *The Natural Alien*, 68.

33. Monika Langer, "Nietzsche, Heidegger, and Merleau-Ponty: Some of Their Contributions and Limitations for 'Environmentalism,'" in *Eco-Phenomenology: Back to the Earth Itself*, ed. Charles S. Brown and Ted Toadvine (Albany: State University of New York Press, 2003), 113.

34. Langer, "Nietzsche, Heidegger, and Merleau-Ponty," 114.

35. Kevin Michael Deluca, "Thinking with Heidegger: Rethinking Environmental Theory and Practice," *Ethics and the Environment* 10, no. 1 (2005): 67–87.

36. Ruth Irwin, *Heidegger, Politics and Climate Change: Risking It All* (New York: Continuum, 2008), 145.

37. Irwin, *Heidegger, Politics and Climate Change*, 150.

38. Ruth Irwin, "Reflections on Modern Climate Change and Finitude," in *Climate Change and Philosophy: Transformational Possibilities*, ed. Ruth Irwin (New York: Continuum, 2010).

39. Bryan Bannon, *From Mastery to Mystery: A Phenomenological Foundation for an Environmental Ethic* (Athens: Ohio University Press, 2014), chapter 4.

40. Bannon, *From Mastery to Mystery*, 151.

41. Martin Heidegger, *What Is a Thing?* trans. W. B. Barton Jr. and Vera Deutsch (Chicago: Henry Regnery Company, 1967), 51 [GA 41, 49].

42. Naess calls Heidegger a "source of inspiration" in *The Ecology of Wisdom: Writings by Arne Naess*, ed. Alan Drengson and Bill Devall (Berkeley: Counterpoint, 2008), 234. Devall and Sessions cite Heidegger as a person who made a significant contribution to the movement in *Deep Ecology: Living As If Nature Mattered* (Layton, Utah: Gibbs M. Smith Inc., 1985), 98–99.

43. Ben Belden Mugula, "The Need for Anthropocentric Approaches vis-à-vis Ecocentric Views in Conservation of Global Renewable Resources," *International Journal of Agricultural Sciences* 3, no. 2 (2013): 384.

44. Henryk Skolimowski, "The Dogma of Anti-Anthropocentrism and Ecophilosophy," *Environmental Ethics* 6, no. 3 (1984): 284.

45. Aldo Leopold, *A Sand County Almanac and Sketches Here and There* (New York: Oxford University Press, 1949), 204.

46. Leopold, *A Sand County Almanac*, 129.

47. Devall and Sessions, *Deep Ecology*, 80. A nice selection of the poetry of Robinson Jeffers is found in *The Wild God of the World: An Anthology of Robinson Jeffers*, ed. Albert Gelpi (Stanford: Stanford University Press, 2003).

48. Heidegger, "The Age of the World Picture," in *The Question Concerning Technology and Other Essays*, trans. William Lovitt (New York: Harper & Row, 1977), 133 [GA 5, 93].

49. Martin Heidegger, *Identity and Difference*, trans. Joan Stambaugh (Chicago and London: The University of Chicago Press, 1969), 31 [GA 11, 39].

50. Martin Heidegger, *Pathmarks*, ed. William McNeill (Cambridge: Cambridge University Press, 1998), 248 [GA 9, 326].

51. Michael E. Zimmerman, "Heidegger's Phenomenology and Contemporary Environmentalism," 73–74.

52. The German word *Wesen* is usually translated as "essence." However, since Heidegger thinks of *Wesen* as an unfolding or happening that is inherent in an entity, I will typically translate the term as "essential unfolding." At times, "essence" is the least awkward translation. I defer to the common translation in such instances.

53. This is not to say that Heidegger discredits such interpretations. He states, for instance, that "'Dasein' can be taken as something which is present-at-hand and just present-at-hand" in *Being and Time*, trans. John Macquarrie and Edward Robinson (New York: Harper & Row, 1962), 82 [GA 2, 75], that is, as an object, though this is "inappropriate to entities of Dasein's character" (*Being and Time*, 67 [GA 2, 56]). Basically, Heidegger is not opposed to scientific categorizations of human beings, but such categorizations are not in line with his project.

54. Heidegger does, however, have a more specific sense of Dasein as human beings in their opening to being, as I will argue below.

55. Thomas Sheehan notes that Heidegger sometimes blurs the distinction between *Dasein* and *Da-sein*. Cf. *Making Sense of Heidegger: A Paradigm Shift* (London and New York: Rowman & Littlefield International, 2015), xvi.

56. Heidegger, *Identity and Difference*, 31 [GA 11, 39].

57. Heidegger, *Pathmarks*, 248 [GA 9, 326].

58. Emmanuel Faye, *Heidegger: The Introduction of Nazism into Philosophy* (New Haven, Conn.: Yale University Press, 2009), 6.

59. Faye, *Heidegger*, 319.

60. Mit Heidegger gegen Heidegger denken. Zur Veröffentlichung von Vorlesungen aus dem Jahre 1935. *Frankfurter Allgemeine Zeitung.* July 25, 1953.

61. Jürgen Habermas, "Work and *Weltanschauung*: The Heidegger Controversy from a German Perspective," in *Heidegger: A Critical Reader*, 187.

62. Heidegger, GA 95, 97.

63. Heidegger, GA 96, 46.

64. Richard Polt and Gregory Fried, "Introduction," in *Nature, History, State: 1933–1934*, trans. Richard Polt and Gregory Fried (London and New York: Bloomsbury, 2013), 1.

65. Michael E. Zimmerman, *Contesting Earth's Future: Radical Ecology and Postmodernity* (Berkeley, Los Angeles, and London: University of California Press, 1994), 6–7.

66. Cf. Michael E. Zimmerman, "Rethinking the Heidegger-Deep Ecology Connection."

67. Peter Staudenmaier, "Fascist Ideology: The 'Green Wing' of the Nazi Party and Its Historical Antecedents," in *Ecofascism: Lessons from the German Experience*, ed. Janet Biehl and Peter Staudenmaier (Edinburgh and San Francisco: AK Press, 1995), 12.

68. Thomas Rohrkrämer, "Martin Heidegger, National Socialism, and Environmentalism," in *How Green Were the Nazis? Nature, Environment, and Nation in the Third Reich*, ed. Franz-Josef Brüggemeier, Mark Cioc, and Thomas Zeller (Athens: Ohio University Press, 2005), 179.

69. Cf. Heidegger's own account of this in "Only a God Can Save Us: *Der Spiegel's* Interview with Martin Heidegger," trans. Maria Alter and John D. Caputo, *Philosophy Today* 20 (1976): 267–284.

70. Martin Heidegger, *Introduction to Metaphysics*, second edition, trans. Gregory Fried and Richard Polt (New Haven and London: Yale University Press, 2014), 68 [GA 40, 47].

71. Gregory Fried, *Heidegger's Polemos: From Being to Politics* (New Haven and London: Yale University Press, 2000), 146.

72. Zimmerman, *Heidegger's Confrontation with Modernity*, 37.

73. As Michael Imort argues, however, much of this was more political rhetoric than political practice since the Nazi war machine required massive resources to sustain. See his "'Eternal Forest—Eternal *Volk*': The Rhetoric and Reality of National Socialist Forest Policy," in *How Green Were the Nazis? Nature, Environment, and Nation in the Third Reich*, ed. Franz-Josef Brüggemeier, Mark Cioc, and Thomas Zeller (Athens: Ohio University Press, 2005), 43–72.

74. Martin Heidegger, *Mindfulness*, trans. Parvis Emad and Thomas Kalary (New York and London: Continuum, 2006), 102–103 [GA 66, 122–123].

75. Martin Heidegger, *Towards the Definition of Philosophy*, trans. Ted Sadler (New York and London: Continuum, 2000), 45 [GA 56/57, 54].

76. Cf. Heidegger, *Identity and Difference*, 34 [GA 11, 43].

77. Cf. Martin Heidegger, *Introduction to Metaphysics*, 219–222 [GA 40, 149–152].

78. Arne Naess, *Ecology, Community and Lifestyle*, trans. and ed. David Rothenberg (Cambridge: Cambridge University Press, 1989), 67.

79. Foltz, *Inhabiting the Earth*, 175.

80. Cf. Immanuel Kant, *Groundwork for the Metaphysics of Morals*, ed. and trans. Allen W. Wood (New Haven and London: Yale University Press, 2002), 46.

81. Cf. Casey Rentmeester, "A Kantian Look at Climate Change," *Essays in Philosophy* 11, no. 1 (2010): 76–86.

Chapter One

Components of the Climate Crisis

Among the many legacies that Martin Heidegger's philosophy leaves is an emphasis on the proper meanings of words. In fact, in his magnum opus, *Being and Time*, Heidegger argues that "the ultimate business of philosophy is to preserve the *force of the most elemental words* in which Dasein expresses itself, and to keep the common understanding from leveling them off to [an] unintelligibility."[1] For Heidegger, words have a force or charge that requires respect, and Dasein—the human being in its openness to being [*Sein*], that is, in its openness to the significance of beings—has a responsibility not only to defer to the meanings of words but also to maintain the forceful nature of words. Above all else, Heidegger stresses the importance of asking the right questions with the proper words. In fact, Heidegger claims "questioning is the genuine and the right and the only way of deeming worthy that which, by its highest rank, holds our Dasein in its power."[2] It is fitting for humans to question not only the world around us, but also our relation to the world. Such questioning does not happen in a vacuum; rather, Heidegger repeatedly emphasizes that human beings are fundamentally social in nature. Since "the world of Dasein is a with-world,"[3] i.e., since humans always share the world with others and thereby question with others, it is important to be open to the proper questions we face as human beings.

As Fried argues, "the principal challenge of Heidegger [is] . . . to respond to questions that arise from the pressing concerns of the world within which we live."[4] Heidegger's corpus includes an impressive array of such questions, including novel interpretations of the experience of technology, science, art, language, and poetry, among others. Importantly, Heidegger argued that all questions arise historically. Since human beings have "facticity,"[5] that is, since human beings are situated in a certain place at a certain time in a certain context, and so forth, the questions that arise are contingent on this place, time,

1

breakdown prompts questions

and context. I argue that the fundamental question that we humans need to ask is as follows: "What is our proper relationship to the natural world?" Heidegger would say that deep questions such as these emerge in situations of breakdown.[6] When things are not going right, fundamental questions arise that there is no point in asking when things are going smoothly. To use one of Heidegger's famous examples, we don't recognize that the hammer we are using is unfit for the job until a problem arises as we use it.[7] Similarly, for most of human history, there was no need to question the human relationship with the natural world since we did not come across breakdowns that initiated basic questioning. Now, however, climate change is an obvious sign of a breakdown concerning the human relationship with nature. Consider recent statements from climatologists and climate philosophers: Lonnie G. Thompson, a world-renowned climatologist, explains the issue of climate change in the starkest of terms: "Global warming poses a clear and present danger to civilization"[8]; Dale Jamieson, one of the first professional philosophers to analyze climate change, argues that climate change requires a paradigm shift in our philosophical approach to the issue[9]; indeed, Martin Schönfeld, a contemporary philosopher who specializes in climate issues, argues that, due to climate change, "culture as we know it must be reinvented, identity as such must be redefined, and reality in its entire environmental gestalt must be reappraised."[10] These are not hyperbolic, apocalyptic ramblings; rather, they reflect the sobering reality of our situation. Put simply, climate change is a sign of a breakdown regarding the human relationship to nature.

With any such breakdown, we do right to find the proper words to understand the situation. The most fitting word that captures our predicament is the ancient Greek word κρίσις [*krisis*], from which we derive our English words "crisis" and "critical." The ancient Greeks understood κρίσις as an unstable pivotal situation that required a decision.[11] For instance, the Greek historian Thucydides speaks of the κρίσιν ἔχειν [*krisin exein*], i.e., the event to be decided, regarding the fate of the Peloponnesian War.[12] As in pivotal situations like wars, human beings have come across a critical juncture regarding our relation to nature, and such a juncture requires a decision as to the appropriate way forward. In his late-1930s work, *Contributions to Philosophy*, among the "decisions" humans have in modernity that Heidegger lists is "whether nature is degraded to the realm of exploitation by means of calculation and ordering"[13] or whether we can embrace a new understanding of the human–nature relationship. If we update this to our present situation, we can say that climate change forces us to make a decision as to the proper way forward: do we continue to exploit the natural world in accordance with the calculative and ordering tendencies of natural science and industry as we have done since the Industrial Revolution or are we able to open up a new relation between humans and nature that is not built upon a conqueror–conquered model?

Ruth Irwin argues that climate change is precisely the sort of breakdown that necessitates a reorientation towards reality. She states, "Backed into a corner by climate change, it is impossible to retain the same ways of doing things that have characterized the last epoch."[14] In facing the real possibility of a collapse of human civilization, Irwin argues that the proper response is to reflect on the finitude of civilization. As she puts it, "In the face of the utter finitude of our world and the concurrent complete loss of meaning, Heidegger draws ultimate strength."[15] Heidegger's philosophy provides us with a lens from which to understand the crisis of climate change insofar as his thought offers an analysis of the conceptual underpinnings in the Western world that have sanctioned environmental destruction. His thought also provides the scaffolding for a new understanding of the proper human–environment relationship. Before we can understand this analysis and Heideggerian framework, though, we need to get a sense as to what the crisis entails.

CLIMATE CHANGE AS A SIGN OF THE CRISIS

While Heidegger would certainly be wary of couching our understanding of climate change in a purely scientific perspective, an elementary comprehension of the science of climate change is essential.[16] Despite the enormity of the problem of climate change, the basic science underlying the phenomenon is simple. Since the Industrial Revolution, humans have increased the amount of greenhouse gases in the atmosphere through their use of fossil fuels and land-use practices. This has resulted in the natural blanket of greenhouse gases that helps keep the earth habitable to thicken, which thereby traps more energy in the climate system, leading to an enhanced greenhouse effect and, ultimately, climate change. Basically, shortwave radiation from the sun enters the earth's atmosphere as it has since the planet has been hospitable to life, but less of the long-wave radiation that is reflected from the earth is able to escape the atmosphere due to the increased thickness of the blanket of greenhouse gases, leading to a more energetic climate. As the human population on the earth increases, so does the use of fossil fuels, the primary means of energy since the Industrial Revolution, which thereby increases the amount of greenhouse gases, further exacerbating the problem. Moreover, more people means more mouths to feed, which requires clearing forests to make way for agriculture, thereby depleting natural carbon sinks. Therefore, the two primary drivers of climate change—fossil fuel use and land alteration—are intensified by an increase in population, much of which is possible due to the scientific and industrial progress resulting from the Industrial Revolution.

While it is undeniable that the Industrial Revolution has provided human beings the opportunity to thrive in certain obvious spheres such as medicine and technology, industrial progress has also sparked the climate crisis. The Intergovernmental Panel on Climate Change (IPCC), which is not only the world's most reputable authority on climate change but also "the largest peer-reviewed scientific collaboration in the history of the world,"[17] states that "warming of the climate system is unequivocal" and that "human influence on the climate system is clear."[18] In other words, there is no longer any serious debate among scientists that climate change is happening, and it is clear that climate change is an anthropogenic, i.e., a human-induced, phenomenon.

The impacts of climate change listed by the IPCC are far-reaching and highly destructive. Among the changes that have already come about are as follows: global warming, rising global sea level, ocean acidification, melting glaciers, lessened crop yields, and an increase in the frequency and severity of extreme weather events, including heat waves, droughts, floods, cyclones, and wildfires.[19] This chronicled devastation has led Bill McKibben, perhaps the foremost environmentalist in the United States, to declare that we rename the planet from Earth to "Eaarth," since it is simply not the same one that our ancestors took for granted. As he puts it, "We're moving quickly from a world where we push nature around to a world where nature pushes back."[20] Fellow environmentalist Lester Brown argues that the world is "on the edge," noting that "no generation has faced a challenge with the complexity, scale, and urgency of the one that we face."[21] Simply put, anthropogenic climate change means a more energetic climate, which is harsher to live in for not only human beings but also the resources and ecosystems that we rely upon. And, as the IPCC reminds us, when we look to the future, the situation will likely only get worse without a drastic change in human behavior: "Continued emission of greenhouse gases will cause further warming and long-lasting changes in all components of the climate system, increasing the likelihood of severe, pervasive and irreversible impacts for people and ecosystems."[22] One of the most obvious effects of climate change on human beings is the impact on the basic necessities humans require in order to live: water, food, and forests. We will therefore begin with an analysis of the impact on resources and then move on to the wider effects of climate change.

RESOURCE DEPLETIONS AND TERRA-TRANSFORMATION IN THE ANTHROPOCENE

Despite the impressive mastery over the natural world that humans have displayed since the Industrial Revolution, it is a simple fact that all humans rely upon the earth's resources to survive. Therefore, substantial deterioration of the resource base is critically problematic for the human species. Climate change can be viewed as a catalyst in that it incites change in our resource base at a fundamental level. The increase in the amount of energy in the atmosphere that thereby leads to global warming has an overall negative effect on the water resources available for human consumption.[23] With warming comes melted ice sheets, which means freshwater that was stored glacially often turns into saltwater as it melts into the oceans. Shrinking mountain glaciers also reduce the availability of freshwater for humans to drink. While the amount of water on the planet basically stays the same, less and less is readily available for human consumption due to climate change.

Since food requires water to grow, water scarcity leads to an overall decrease in crop yields. Other effects of climate change are also detrimental to food supplies: heat waves, droughts, floods, and wildfires that result from global warming significantly lessen crop production in general. Trees are affected in the same negative fashion, and deforestation is especially problematic in regard to climate change since deforestation causes carbon dioxide—the deadliest greenhouse gas—to be released from the trees into the atmosphere, which only intensifies the enhanced greenhouse effect since it turns a natural carbon sink into a source of greenhouse gas. In all, the essential resource base that humans rely upon for survival is depleting quickly, thereby leading scientists to question the long-term stability of human civilizations as we have come to know them. James Hansen, perhaps the most eminent climatologist in the world, states, "Life will survive, but it will do so on a transformed planet. For all foreseeable human generations, it will be a far more desolate world than the one in which civilization developed and flourished during the past several thousand years."[24] If climate change can be viewed as the catalyst, resource base deterioration can be seen as one of the resultant effects.

Since nonhuman animals are also dependent on these resources for survival, the deteriorating resource foundation is clearly detrimental to nonhuman animal species. In fact, we are currently experiencing what scientists are calling "the Sixth Extinction." In categorizing extinctions, scientists use the term "background extinction rate" to refer to the rate expected given natural variations. Mass extinctions occur when the there is an extinction of a "significant proportion of the world's biota in a geologically insignificant amount of time."[25] Unlike the previous five mass extinctions that have occurred in the history of the planet caused by events such as asteroid impact on the earth or unmitigated volcanic activity in the earth's crust, the Sixth Extinction is primarily caused by human beings. Anthony Darnosky et al. explain the Sixth Extinction as follows: "Humans are now causing the sixth mass extinction through co-opting resources, fragmenting habitats, introducing non-native species, spreading pathogens, killing species directly, and changing global climate."[26] This list of causes can be compressed into three categories, all of which are related and primarily anthropogenic: climate change, resource base deterioration, and terra-transformation.[27] The category of terra-transformation includes both direct and indirect alteration of the earth's landscapes and ecosystems, much of which is made possible by industrialization. Biologist Anthony Ricciardi makes the following claim regarding the ubiquity of the human transformation of the planet:

> Although species invasions have pervaded the history of life and have periodically occurred in waves after geographic barriers have been lifted, such events differ markedly from human-assisted invasions in spatial and temporal scales and in the diversity of organisms involved in long-distance dispersal. These were episodic phenomena involving only neighboring regions and small fractions of the species. . . . By contrast, the current human-driven mass invasion event is global in scale and likely to be continuous through the remainder of human history.[28]

The tripartite human influence on other species that includes climate change, resource depletions, and terra-transformation is simply too much for many species to handle. While humans have technological means to stave off some of the negative impacts in the short term, the remainder of earth's species must rely upon evolutionary adaptation. However, since the changes are so rapid, species are unable to adapt. Elizabeth Kolbert, author of *The Sixth Extinction*, provides this clear synopsis: "When the world changes faster than species can adapt, many fall out."[29] Perhaps what is most thought provoking is what is in store for humanity if many of the species that we coinhabit the earth with die off, as Kolbert notes with the following commentary: "having freed ourselves from the constraints of evolution, humans nevertheless remain dependent on the earth's biological and geochemical systems. By disrupting these systems—cutting down tropical rainforests, altering the composition of the atmosphere, acidifying the oceans—we're putting our own survival in danger."[30]

The human influence on the environment has been so impactful that scientists have come to call the period beginning in the late eighteenth century the "Anthropocene," or "the epoch of humans." Scientist Paul Crutzen, who coined the term "Anthropocene," calls the human race "a major environmental force."[31] Along with his fellow colleagues, he explains the Anthropocene as follows:

> Although Earth has undergone many periods of significant environmental change, the planet's environment has been unusually stable for the past 10,000 years. This period of stability—known to geologists as the Holocene—has seen

human civilizations arise, develop and thrive. Such stability may now be under threat. Since the Industrial Revolution, a new era has arisen, the Anthropocene, in which human actions have become the main driver of global environmental change.[32]

We humans are not simply one animal species among others; rather, we have been the foremost environmental force for the past three centuries. Although the typical scale of geological epochs is on the order of tens of millions of years, human behaviors in the past few centuries have had such a transformative and ubiquitous impact that they are of *geological* significance. This planetary impact provides us with an opportunity to step back and reflect on the proper human relationship to the rest of the natural world. A proper reflection questions the appropriate *place* of human beings in juxtaposition with nature, and this leads us into the question of whether our approach to environmentalism should be anthropocentric or not.

The anthropocentrism–antianthropocentrism debate has formed so much of the discourse of environmental philosophy that it can be said to form a party line.[33] Using an insight from Garrett Hardin's classic paper, "The Tragedy of the Commons" from 1968, I argue that this debate is now in a certain sense moot. Hardin's essay deals primarily with the problem of overpopulation and its link to pollution. His overall argument is that the human overpopulation problem cannot be solved by technological or political means. Within the argument, he provides this important insight:

> The pollution problem is a consequence of population. It did not much matter how a lonely American frontiersman disposed of his waste. "Flowing water purifies itself every 10 miles," my grandfather used to say, and the myth was near enough to the truth when he was a boy, for there were not too many people. But as population became denser, the natural chemical and biological recycling processes became overloaded.[34]

He goes on to argue that morality itself is "system-sensitive," i.e., dependent upon the way things are. This implies that the same action could be perfectly moral in one context and immoral in another. If our moral stance should be informed by the way the world *is*, then we should be cognizant of the state of things if we are to respond in an appropriate manner.

Philosophers in the Western tradition tend to distinguish the way the world *is* from the way the world *ought to be*. They argue that this distinction, often referred to as "Hume's guillotine," must not only be kept in mind, but also should be completely severed since descriptive claims and prescriptive claims are different types of entities. Hume states, as compared to *is* or *is not*, "*ought*, or *ought not*, expresses some new relation or affirmation" and thus it is "inconceivable how this new relation can be a deduction from [*is* or *is not*], which are entirely different from it."[35] In other words, there is nothing about the way the world *is* that precludes us from determining the way the world *ought* to be. While it is true that descriptive claims and prescriptive claims are different types of entities, we would be amiss to think that the way the world is has no bearing on the way the world ought to be. If it is the case—and it *is*—that human beings are clearly different from other species in their capacity to change the environment, then we should not aspire to an ethic that makes us "plain members and citizens" of the biotic community, as Aldo Leopold, the most famous proponent of antianthropocentric environmentalism, would have us do. To do so would simply be unrealistic. Instead, we should use the knowledge of how things are to develop an ethic that is cognizant of the special status of human beings. The fact that humans change the environment in ways that are *geologically* significant, as evidenced by the devastating effects of climate change in the Anthropocene, means that we need to craft an ethic that is cognizant of this uniqueness.

A HEIDEGGERIAN RESPONSE

In the field of environmental philosophy, most approaches to climate change have taken on this issue from a traditional ethical standpoint. I have tried to show in the past what a deontological approach to climate change would look like, and others have tackled the issue from a utilitarian perspective.[36] Recently, I have argued that a nontheoretical "Do No Harm" principle that essentially says one should not knowingly harm other living human beings unnecessarily may be an appropriate response.[37] However, I have come to the realization that such approaches are not truly reflective of the severity of the situation. As Schönfeld argues, we need to move from climate ethics to climate philosophy.[38] While climate ethics is the theoretical enterprise of applying ethical principles to the climate crisis, climate philosophy asks deeper questions about the human relationship with the natural world and the ways in which we encounter natural entities. Given Heidegger's emphasis on the importance of questioning, his philosophy is appropriately positioned to provide us with an appropriate starting point.

In the initial mining of the Heidegger–environmentalism connection, Zimmerman showed how Heidegger could be seen as a forerunner to the movement of deep ecology. In his founding work on deep ecology, Naess makes a distinction between shallow and deeper approaches to environmentalism. While shallow ecology's goal is to increase the health and affluence of human beings by managing resources efficiently and curbing pollution, deep ecology questions the assumptions that have led to the environmental crisis in the first place.[39] Although Heidegger's emphasis on questioning assumptions is clearly in line with the overall project of deep ecology, some aspects of deep ecology are certainly not amenable to Heidegger's thought. For instance, while most deep ecologists consider biospherical egalitarianism to be an ideal we need to pursue in principle, Heidegger's emphasis on the uniqueness of the human being is at odds with such a conception. Zimmerman eventually realizes the incompatibility of deep ecology and Heidegger's philosophy in 1993 when he notes that "deep ecologists are sometimes suspicious of Heidegger's claims about the uniqueness of humanity's capacity for understanding being."[40] Following Hardin's insight, I propose that we take heed of the present situation as we attempt to find a way to respond appropriately to the environmental crisis. Given the fact that we live in the Anthropocene wherein human beings are easily the most destructive planetary force, our response should be cognizant of humanity's uniqueness. Thus, Heidegger's human exceptionalism, which was once considered to be a detriment to his philosophy in environmental circles, should now be considered an asset. In fact, Heidegger's elucidation of the uniqueness of the human being is helpful in understanding just how humans have become so environmentally destructive.

Human beings are unique from the Heideggerian perspective because we are open to the ways in which things manifest themselves *as* what they are. Heidegger argues that Dasein stands in a clearing [*Lichtung*] or open space in which entities can show up as mattering in one way or another.[41] In fact, Heidegger argues that "'*There is*' ['*Es gibt*'] *truth only insofar as Dasein is and as long as Dasein is*. Entities are uncovered only *when* Dasein *is*; and only as long as Dasein *is*, are they disclosed."[42] This does not mean that human beings decide what it means for something to *be*; rather, it means that without Dasein, entities would not show up as meaningful. Frederick Olafson notes that for Heidegger nonhuman animals do not interpret entities *as* entities since they do not have language.[43] Herein lies a fundamental difference between humans and animals. Although Heidegger states that it is a "great difficulty . . . to make out what is given to animals as living beings and how the given is unveiled for them,"[44] he does argue at one point that nonhuman animals lack an ability to encounter an entity *as* an entity. For instance, he states, "The blade of grass that the beetle crawls up, for example, is not a blade of grass for it at all; it is not something possibly destined to become part of the bundle of hay with which the peasant will feed his cow."[45] This fundamental difference has immense consequences. While nonhuman animals can certainly affect ecosystems in negative ways, they cannot transform the world into their own image. Only a human being is able to do this since a human being is open to the ways in which entities emerge and therefore can take entities in different ways. For instance, only humans can transform their understanding of the woods into a forest of timber, the mountain into a quarry of rock, and the river into waterpower.[46]

Using Heidegger's example of the beetle as a cue, we can say that a species of beetles can be accidentally introduced into an ecosystem with no natural predators and wreak havoc on certain species of grass, thereby disrupting the balance of an ecosystem (as the Japanese beetle has done, for instance, in parts of the United States). Regardless of how destructive an invasive species of beetle might be, however, the destruction is fundamentally different than the type of destruction done by human beings. Given the human being's distinctive status as language beings, a human can consciously rework the very same grass in accordance with his or her own interests. On a much larger scale, Heidegger would say that only a human being can interpret nature *as* "an energy source for modern technology and industry."[47] In fact, Heidegger argues that this is precisely the way in which nature comes to be encountered during what he calls the age of modern technology. Here, "everywhere everything is ordered to stand by, to be immediately at hand, indeed to stand there just so that it may be on call for a further ordering. Whatever is ordered about in this way has its own standing. We call it the standing-reserve [*Bestand*]."[48] When nature becomes standing-reserve, it becomes an undifferentiated grid of energy on hand for human purposes. Heidegger provides the following examples to show how nature *as* standing-reserve shows up to human beings: "The earth now reveals itself as a coal mining district, the soil as a mineral deposit,"[49] "agriculture is now the mechanized food industry,"[50] and "nature becomes a gigantic gasoline station."[51] In the age of modern technology, everything shows up for human beings as opportunities for exploitation such that entities no longer have any standing of their own. This ability to take entities *as* mere resources for human consumption and rework them in accordance with human interests is a uniquely human activity from the Heideggerian perspective, and this uniquely human activity allows for environmental destruction that is simply of a different order than what one may find produced by nonhuman animals.

Heidegger's way of characterizing how entities appear in the age of modern technology is one of his novel contributions to phenomenology. The ultimate task of phenomenology is to describe what appears to us *as* it appears to us. As Charles Guignon notes, phenomena means "what 'shows itself,' what 'becomes manifest' or 'shows forth' *for us*, in relation to our purposes as they are shaped by our forms of life."[52] Heidegger's mentor, Edmund Husserl, famously provides the slogan "to the things themselves"[53] for phenomenology, and Heidegger cites this slogan in *Being and Time*.[54] Heidegger uses phenomenology as his method of ontology, that is, as his method of studying the being of entities. Importantly, the way in which entities show up is historical from Heidegger's perspective. The understanding of reality that reigns in the age of modern technology is not the same as the understanding that dominated previous periods of history, which Heidegger calls "epochs." However, as Heidegger argues, "there is a legacy [*Überlieferung*] from epoch to epoch."[55] The German word *Überlieferung* commonly means "tradition" and comes from the verb *überliefern*, meaning "to hand down" or "pass along." Therefore, the understanding of reality in the age of modern technology has its roots in the Western metaphysical tradition. Following the common understanding of the history of Western philosophy and thus metaphysics, Heidegger argues this tradition originates in ancient Greece. He states, "We constantly return to the Greek conception of being because this conception, though entirely flattened out and rendered unrecognizable, is the conception that still rules even today in the West—not only in the doctrines of philosophy but in the most everyday routines."[56] In order to understand our current understanding of being wherein entities are encountered as standing-reserve, then, we must trace the legacy of Western metaphysics. In terms of eco-phenomenology, our task will be to trace the Western understanding of nature since this question is enmeshed in how we experience the world as a whole. Situated in terms of the basic question I aim to pose— "What is our proper relationship to the natural world?"—we must first trace the legacy of Western metaphysics to understand how we should properly answer this question in response to the environmental crisis we face.

NOTES

1. Martin Heidegger, *Being and Time*, 262 [GA 2, 291].
2. Martin Heidegger, *Introduction to Metaphysics*, 91 [GA 40, 63].
3. Heidegger, *Being and Time*, 155 [GA 2, 159].
4. Gregory Fried, "Heidegger, Politics, and Us: Towards a Polemical Ethics," *Philosophy and Social Criticism* 39, no. 9 (2013): 863.
5. Cf. Heidegger, *Being and Time*, 82 [GA 2, 75].
6. Cf. Heidegger, *Being and Time*, paragraph 16 [GA 2, 97–102].
7. Heidegger, *Being and Time*, 200 [GA 2, 209].
8. Lonnie G. Thompson, "Climate Change: The Evidence and Our Options," *The Behavior Analyst* 33, no. 2 (2010): 153.
9. Dale Jamieson, "Ethics, Public Policy, and Global Warming," *Science, Technology, and Human Values* 17, no. 2 (1992): 148–149.
10. Martin Schönfeld, "Ecosophy in the Climate Age," *Zhexue Wenhua* 39, no. 7 (2012): 69–90.
11. Henry George Liddell and Robert Scott, *An Intermediate Greek-English Lexicon* (Oxford: Clarendon Press, 2003), 451.
12. Thucydides, *The Peloponnesian War*, translated by Steven Lattimore (Indianapolis: Hackett Publishing, 1998), 294–301.
13. Martin Heidegger, *Contributions to Philosophy (From Enowning)*, trans. Parvis Emad and Kenneth Maly (Bloomington and Indianapolis: Indiana University Press, 1999), 63 [GA 65, 91].

14. Irwin, *Heidegger, Politics and Climate Change: Risking It All* (New York: Continuum, 2008), 149.

15. Irwin, *Heidegger, Politics and Climate Change*, 148. Irwin is dealing explicitly with Heidegger's work "On the Question of Being," in *Pathmarks*, 291–322 [GA 9, 385–426]. In this work, Heidegger is dealing specifically with Ernst Jünger's text, *Über die Linie*, in which Jünger provides a meditation on nihilism. This meditation is not so much about the collapse of civilization but rather the collapse of meaning that accompanies technological nihilism. Nevertheless, her insight that climate change ignites a crisis in philosophy is both fitting and original.

16. Heidegger's philosophy of science will be examined at length in chapter 3.

17. Lisa Heinzerling, "Climate Change, Human Health, and the Post-Cautionary Principle," *Georgetown Law Journal* 96, no. 2 (2008): 457.

18. IPCC, "Summary for Policymakers," in *Climate Change 2014: Impacts, Adaptation, and Vulnerability. Part A: Global and Sectoral Aspects. Contribution of Working Group II to the Fifth Assessment Report of the Intergovernmental Panel on Climate Change*, ed. C. B. Field et al. (Cambridge and New York: Cambridge University Press, 2014), 1.

19. IPCC, "Summary for Policymakers," 1–8.

20. Bill McKibben, *Eaarth: Making a Life on a Tough New Planet* (New York: Henry Holt and Company, 2010), 101.

21. Lester R. Brown, *World on the Edge: How to Prevent Environmental and Economic Collapse* (New York and London: W.W. Norton and Company, 2011), xi.

22. IPCC, "Summary for Policymakers," 8.

23. IPCC, "Summary for Policymakers," 17.

24. James Hansen, "The Threat to the Planet," *New York Review of Books*, July 2006, 12.

25. A. Hallam and P. B. Wignall, *Mass Extinctions and Their Aftermath* (Oxford: Oxford University Press, 1997), 1.

26. Anthony D. Barnosky et al., "Has the Earth's Sixth Mass Extinction Already Arrived?" *Nature* 471, no. 7336 (2011): 51.

27. I use the term "terra-transformation" instead of the popular term "terraformation" to highlight the fact that we are not simply forming the earth from a blank slate but rather *trans*forming an earth that already had an evolutionary structure of its own. Terraformation also sometimes refers to the hypothetical process of forming planets to be suitable to human beings, which is clearly not the same as altering Earth itself.

28. Anthony Ricciardi, "Are Modern Biological Invasions an Unprecedented Form of Global Change?" *Conservation Biology* 21, no. 2 (2007): 334.

29. Elizabeth Kolbert, *The Sixth Extinction: An Unnatural History* (New York: Henry Holt and Company, 2014), 266.

30. Kolbert, *The Sixth Extinction*, 267.

31. Paul J. Crutzen, "Geology of Mankind," *Nature* 415, no. 6867 (2002): 23.

32. Johan Rockström et al., "A Safe Operating Space for Humanity," *Nature* 461, no. 7263 (2009): 472.

33. Cf. Skolimowski, "The Dogma of Anti-Anthropocentrism and Ecophilosophy."

34. Garrett Hardin, "The Tragedy of the Commons," *Science* 162, no. 3859 (1968): 1245.

35. David Hume, *A Treatise of Human Nature*, ed. David Fate Norton and Mary J. Norton (New York: Oxford University Press, 2000), 300.

36. Cf. Casey Rentmeester, "A Kantian Look at Climate Change" and John Broome, *Climate Matters: Ethics in a Warming World* (New York: W.W. Norton, 2012).

37. Casey Rentmeester, "Do No Harm: A Cross-Disciplinary, Cross-Cultural Climate Ethics," *De Ethica* 1, no. 2 (2014): 5–22.

38. Martin Schönfeld, "From Climate Ethics to Climate Philosophy," *Climate Philosophy Newsletter* 4, no. 1 (2010): 22–27.

39. Naess, "The Shallow and the Deep, Long-Range Ecological Movement."

40. Zimmerman, "Rethinking the Heidegger-Deep Ecology Relationship," 201.

41. Cf. Heidegger, *Being and Time*, 171 [GA 2, 177].

42. Heidegger, *Being and Time*, 269 [GA 2, 299].

43. Frederick A. Olafson, *Heidegger and the Philosophy of Mind* (New Haven, Conn.: Yale University Press, 1987), 68.

44. Martin Heidegger, *The Basic Problems of Phenomenology*, revised edition, trans. Albert Hofstadter (Bloomington and Indianapolis: Indiana University Press, 1982), 190 [GA 24, 270].

45. Martin Heidegger, *Fundamental Concepts of Metaphysics: World, Finitude, Solitude*, trans. William McNeil and Nicholas Walker (Bloomington: Indiana University Press, 1995), 198 [GA 29/30, 291].

46. Cf. Heidegger, *Being and Time*, 100 [GA 2, 95].

47. Martin Heidegger, *Discourse on Thinking*, trans. John M. Anderson and E. Hans Fruend (New York, Hagerstown, San Francisco, and London: Harper & Row, 1966), 50 [GA 16, 523].

48. Martin Heidegger, "The Question Concerning Technology," in *The Question Concerning Technology and Other Essays*, trans. William Lovitt (New York: Harper & Row, 1977), 17 [GA 7, 17].

49. Heidegger, "The Question Concerning Technology," 14 [GA 7, 15].

50. Heidegger, "The Question Concerning Technology," 15 [GA 7, 16].

51. Heidegger, *Discourse on Thinking*, 50 [GA 16, 523].

52. Charles Guignon, "Introduction," in *The Cambridge Companion to Heidegger*, ed. Charles Guignon (Cambridge: Cambridge University Press, 1993), 6.

53. Edmund Husserl, *Logical Investigations*, second edition, trans. and ed. Dermot Moran (London: Routledge, 2001), 168.

54. Heidegger, *Being and Time*, 50 [GA 2, 37].

55. Martin Heidegger, *The Principle of Reason*, trans. Reginald Lilly (Bloomington: Indiana University Press, 1991), 91 [GA 10, 135].

56. Martin Heidegger, *Introduction to Metaphysics*, 64–65 [GA 40, 45].

Chapter Two

Heidegger's History of Being[1]

Our fundamental task lies in attempting to understand how nature came to be viewed as an undifferentiated grid of energy on hand to be maximally exploited. In order to do this, we will utilize Heidegger's history of being [*Seinsgeschichte*] and follow Heidegger's thesis that "the desolation of the earth [stems] from metaphysics."[2] If we apply this thought to our times, we can say that the environmental crisis is a result of our metaphysics. Heidegger puts this point the following way: "Metaphysics is in all its forms and historical stages a unique, but perhaps necessary, fate of the West and the presupposition of its planetary dominance."[3] In other words, the very way in which we understand, interpret, and experience reality has led to the human domination of the planet, which has thereby led to our environmental crisis. In order to make any change in the human–nature relationship, we must look at how the current Western metaphysical outlook has come about by looking at its history, since our current epoch of being stems from earlier epochs. In speaking of Heidegger's understanding of metaphysics, Guignon notes, "Since the first beginning [in ancient Greece] has predefined all subsequent ways of experiencing things, it follows that the historically shifting interpretations of being in our culture have all been permutations on the understanding that took shape at the dawn of our civilization."[4] We will begin with the ancient Greek epoch of being, move into the medieval period, and then examine the modern epoch, since these are the three major epochs of being for Heidegger.[5]

By distinguishing three separate epochs of being in the history of the Western world, Heidegger is pointing out that the humans who lived in these separate epochs lived in different worlds. In *Being and Time*, Heidegger defines "world" as "that '*wherein*' a factical Dasein as such can be said to 'live.'"[6] As Hubert Dreyfus notes, Heidegger's sense of world does not mean the totality of entities on the planet; rather, it has more to do with a web of meaningful relations in which a person dwells in a particular sphere. Dreyfus states, "This sense of world is reflected in such locutions as 'the child's world,' 'the world of fashion,' or 'the business world' (this, as opposed to one's place of business, is what one is 'in' when one is in business)."[7] If we think about world in these terms, it is easy to see how one may live in a different world than another person even if they live down the street from each other. The college student whose days are filled with lectures, studying, and completing assignments is living in a much different world in the Heideggerian sense than the paramedic who spends his days in high-stress, emergency situations, since the things that matter most to the student *qua* student are much different than the things that matter most to the paramedic *qua* paramedic. In other words, the totality of meaningful relations of the student as a student is much different than the totality of meaningful relations of the paramedic as a paramedic. At the same time, however, the student and the paramedic may participate in a shared world in that they may both root for the city's sports team or belong to the same political party.

While we can find some basis for comparison between the student and the paramedic at some level, such a comparison would be more difficult if we were to compare people living in different epochs of being, since the very way in which they experience and interpret entities as a whole is different. As Thomas Wartenberg notes, "In different historical epochs, different worlds reveal themselves, that is, being manifests itself in culturally specific ways to the peoples of such epochs."[8] Keeping this in mind, we can say (for example) that the ancient Greek farmer, the peasant farmer in medieval Europe, and the modern-day farmer all live in different worlds, even if they harvest the same crop, because the ways in which entities show up *as* the entities that they are is different in each period. The ancient Greek farmer may view the crop as a gift of the goddess Demeter, the medieval farmer may view the crop as a creation of the Christian God, and the modern-day farmer may view the crop mainly in terms of its monetary value. Even if we can say that the crop is the same crop, i.e., has the same basic DNA structure, it is viewed in different ways in the various historical epochs, because the people in these epochs live in different worlds. At the same time, however, there are certain constants that bind these worlds together. A healthy, flourishing crop to the Greek, medieval, and modern farmer exhibits the same basic features in all epochs even if this flourishing is understood on different terms. Whether the flourishing is attributed to the grace of Demeter or the Christian God or is simply attributed to a good harvest and is seen in natural terms, certain aspects of what makes the crop a good crop are invariant throughout the worlds.

Heidegger stresses that people living in different epochs live in different worlds, but also notes that there is some thread of consistency between the epochs. He states, "The epochs suddenly spring up like sprouts. The epochs can never be derived from one another much less be placed on the track of an ongoing process [*durchlaufenden Prozesses*]."[9] Heidegger understands a process as a series of events with a determined order. While epochal transitions are not processual in nature, there is an element of "handing down" that occurs from epoch to epoch in that certain concepts from one epoch attain a new emphasis in the subsequent epoch, yet this new emphasis stills carries with it elements of the previous epoch. In order to understand the metaphysical underpinnings of our current epoch of being, then, we must understand the previous epochs of being, what separates the different epochs, and what binds them together.

THE ANCIENT GREEK EPOCH OF BEING

In line with the standard understanding of philosophy in the West, Heidegger points to ancient Greece as the beginning of Western metaphysics and philosophy. The ancient Greeks are the first metaphysicians in the West because they were the first to ask the question, "What *are* beings?" In other words, they were the first to ask what it means *to be* anything whatsoever. The initial answer that the Greeks gave to this question was φύσις [*physis*]. Heidegger states, "In the age of the first and definitive unfolding of Western philosophy among the Greeks, when questioning about beings as such and as a whole received its true inception, beings were called φύσις."[10] Though we usually translate the Greek word φύσις, from which the English word "physics" is derived, as "nature,"[11] Heidegger points out that the early Greeks did not understand φύσις in the same way that we understand nature. For the Greeks, φύσις was the name for what *is*. He states, "What is, as such and as a whole, the Greeks call φύσις,"[12] and Heidegger defines φύσις as "what emerges from itself (for example, the emergence, the blossoming, of a rose), the unfolding that opens itself up, the coming-into-appearance in such unfolding, and holding itself and persisting in appearance—in short, the emerging-abiding sway."[13] Here, we should point out that there are at least two aspects to φύσις: emerging *and* abiding. The emerging into presence itself is φύσις, but *that which emerges*, as an abiding (i.e., *enduring*) entity, is φύσις as well. Heidegger notes that this second aspect of φύσις, what we can call "enduring presence," is the one that philosophers since Plato have emphasized in the West, while the emerging aspect of φύσις has been forgotten.[14] In other words, philosophers have come to focus on *what* comes to presence and have taken for granted the act of *presencing itself*. Heidegger states, "since the dawn of thinking 'being' names the presencing of what is present,"[15] yet the "oblivion of being" soon sets in, and philosophers only emphasize what is present (beings) and forget the presencing of what is present (the being of beings).[16]

The distinction between what is present and presencing itself is Heidegger's famous ontological difference between beings and being.[17] "Beings" is the common translation of the German word *das Seiende*, which literally means "that which is."[18] A being in this sense is any entity whatsoever, whether it be something that actually exists or is imaginary. "Being," which is the translation of the German word *Sein*, is a more difficult concept in Heidegger's philosophy. Heidegger states, "Whenever [one] speaks of beings, the tiny word 'is' names the *being* of beings."[19] I will follow Polt in equating the being of beings with "the multifarious ways in which beings as such can have significance for us, or make a difference to us."[20] In other words, being can be understood roughly as the significance of beings. While Heidegger insists that one must always keep in mind the distinction between beings and being, he understands that they are ultimately inseparable. For instance, in *Being and Time*, he states that "being is always the being of an entity"[21] and in *The Basic Problems of Phenomenology*, he states that "the ontological difference says: A being is always characterized by a specific constitution of being."[22] Here, we can see the interdependence of being and beings: being is dependent on beings, and beings are also dependent on being. However, as humans begin to focus on beings, they forget the very presencing that allows beings to come into unconcealment, and this leads to what Heidegger calls "the forgetfulness of being" [*Seinsvergessenheit*]. He states, "Everywhere we are underway amid beings, and yet we no longer know how it stands with being. We do not even know that we no longer know it."[23] If we want to put this in terms of forgetfulness, we can say that we have not only forgotten the question of being, but we have even forgotten that we have forgotten it.

Heidegger spent his entire adult life trying to revive the question of being [*Seinsfrage*], which at one point in his oeuvre he calls his "one and only question."[24] The revival of this question is the key to halting the "unrestrained exploitation of the earth as a source of raw materials."[25] Consider the following passage from Heidegger's commentary on a fragment from the pre-Socratic philosopher Anaximander: "Man has already begun to overwhelm the entire earth and its atmosphere [and] to arrogate to himself in forms of energy the concealed powers of nature . . . This same defiant man is utterly at a loss simply to say what *is*; to say *what* this *is*—that a thing *is*."[26] Here, Heidegger implies that humans in the contemporary age are no longer open to the question of being, and a revival of this very question is crucial if we wish to change the human–nature relationship. As opposed to our current epoch that has "forgotten" being, the early ancient Greek philosophers had a glimpse into the question of being. Heidegger states that pre-Socratic philosophers like Parmenides, Anaximander, and Heraclitus were able to briefly gain insight into the being of beings in the sense that they questioned the very presencing of beings itself, but this insight and element of wonder was soon covered over by subsequent philosophers who emphasized beings instead of being. The Greeks who came after the pre-Socratic philosophers quickly focused on what endures in presence in their answer to the question "What are beings?" and this emphasis on enduring presence has marked all of Western metaphysics since. Heidegger states, "Since long ago, that which is present has been regarded as what is."[27] While all epochs of being in the Western world see presence as fundamental, *what each epoch understood as what is present differs*, and this is what separates the epochs of being.

Relating this back to the Greeks, the initial word used for being was φύσις in the twofold sense of emerging into presence *and* enduring or abiding presence. For the Greeks, to be an entity eventually means to be something that stands on its own in enduring presence.[28] The key point here is that the Greeks understood beings as entities that *endured of themselves*, i.e., endured of their own accord. Among the various examples of such entities are "a star and a plant, an animal, a human being and a god."[29] According to Heidegger, a particular understanding of being takes form after the pre-Socratics. He states:

> For the Greeks "being" says *constancy* in a twofold sense:
> 1. standing-in-itself as arising and standing forth (φύσις).
> 2. but, as such, "constantly," that is, enduringly, abiding (οὐσία).[30]

As we pointed out, the Greeks start to focus on what is enduringly present in their answer to the question of being, and this constancy is understood in terms of οὐσία [*ousia*].[31] Heidegger states, "οὐσία means being in the sense of constant presence, presence at hand."[32] As enduring presence, οὐσία is interpreted differently by the two greatest philosophers among the Greeks: Plato and Aristotle.

Plato understands οὐσία *as* ἰδέα [*idea*] or εἶδος [*eidos*], which Heidegger claims "rules over all Western thinking, throughout the history of its changes up to today."[33] Ἰδέα and εἶδος, Heidegger argues, mean "not only what we can see with our physical eyes, but everything that can be apprehended. *What any given being is consists in its look, and the look, in turn, presents the being's whatness (allows it to come to presence).*"[34] In other words, the εἶδος or outward look is *formed* into the metaphysical category of the ἰδέα or Form. Plato makes ἰδέα/εἶδος into a metaphysical category with his famous theory of the Forms wherein the Form is an abstract, universal, intellectual blueprint different from but related to the sensuous particular things themselves.[35] Heidegger states:

Plato distinguishes between . . . the being that is in being and also *that* kind of "being" that should not be, or should not be called such. The . . . being that is in being, being proper, that is, being that is in accordance with the essence of being, is εἶδος, the outward appearance in which something shows its form, its ἰδέα, that is, what something is, *whatness*. [*That* kind of "being"] is also in being and accordingly also presents itself—thought in a Greek way—also shows an outward appearance and form, an εἶδος, but the form is warped and twisted . . . [in that] they must show themselves in the form of sensuous matter.[36]

For Plato, the abstract, intellectual, universal realm is what is most real, since it is eternal and therefore enduring; the particular, sensuous realm is always secondary since it is fleeting. Heidegger argues that this distinction between what comes to be called the true and the apparent worlds allows for metaphysics in the Western world, since it makes room for a realm beyond (μετά) physical entities (τὰ φυσικά).[37] We can add that this Platonic conception goes beyond φύσις as well in that the intellectual realm of the Forms is a step away from things as they unfold on their own terms. Instead of apprehending the particular blossoming rose in the fullest sense of φύσις, that is, as *emerging and abiding*, for instance, Plato focuses on the abiding as an instantiation of the enduringly present Form of "roseness." The particular rose, as an entity that emerges and develops, withers, and finally decays, is fleeting and therefore "less real" than the Form of "roseness," which "resides" eternally in a supersensory realm available to the human mind.

Although chronologically Plato comes before Aristotle, Heidegger argues that Aristotle is closer to the pre-Socratics than Plato in his understanding of being.[38] Heidegger states, for Aristotle, "Ἰδέα means nothing other than 'look' (a front against *Plato*): . . . not as though it exists somewhere in a supersensory way, but rather the outline as it shows itself."[39] Since Aristotle understands ἰδέα/εἶδος as simply the look or form of an entity rather than an eternal intellectual blueprint, his philosophy is, to a certain extent, "less metaphysical" than Plato. However, because Aristotle is reacting against Plato's understanding of οὐσία as ἰδέα, he is simultaneously more entrenched in metaphysical thinking than the pre-Socratics.[40] Heidegger claims that Aristotle struggles with two understandings of φύσις, one wider sense that is close to the pre-Socratic notion of the emergence into presence of entities and one that is much more narrow in that it is simply "*one kind of* οὐσία."[41] The primordial, wider sense of φύσις turns out to be a mere *echo* of the pre-Socratic understanding for Aristotle, and he instead takes οὐσία as his primary word for being. Here, φύσις *as* emerging and abiding is degraded in that Aristotle homes in on a specific understanding of φύσις as a type of οὐσία, namely, beings that move or produce themselves.[42] Heidegger situates this specific sense of φύσις in Aristotelian teleology where entities strive towards some τέλος *[telos]* or end. For instance, the blossoming rose has φύσις not in the wide sense that it is emerging into presence but in the narrow sense that it is moving toward an end that is already "in" itself. We can understand this sense of movement as "self-production." Whereas φύσει ὄντα [*physei onta*] (natural entities) are self-produced, τέχνη ὄντα [*techne onta*] (technological entities) are produced by human planning and production.[43] Both, however, are types *of* οὐσία.

While φύσις plays a significant role in the thought of Aristotle, οὐσία is the most basic word for being for Aristotle. In speaking of the way in which Aristotle understood this term, Heidegger states, "οὐσία is, terminologically, 'a being in the how of its being.' . . . Οὐσία is a being that is *there for me in an emphatic way*, in such a way that I can use it, that it is at my disposal . . . The how of being refers to *being there in the manner of being-available*."[44]

In everyday parlance, "οὐσία means property, possession, possessions and goods, estate"[45] in the ancient Greek world, and Heidegger stresses that although Aristotle stipulates οὐσία to mean the *being* of beings, the customary understanding of οὐσία "exists constantly and simultaneously alongside the terminological meaning."[46] Therefore, we can say that οὐσία has a mark of human relationality in that beings are encountered from a human perspective. Heidegger argues that "οὐσία is the abbreviation for παρουσία, 'being-present.'"[47] Given that the customary meaning lingers with this terminological meaning, we can say that οὐσία means being-present in relation *to me*, or at least in relation to the human being. In this sense, Aristotle's understanding of οὐσία is similar to Plato's in that both consider being to be relational to the human being. The difference is that Plato concocts a theoretical realm of the Forms for οὐσία, while Aristotle denies that any such realm needs to be posited. Nevertheless, both fixate on being as οὐσία rather than φύσις. From Heidegger's perspective, "it is from this basic Western determination (initially still genuinely as οὐσία) . . . that all modifications of the interpretation of beings ensue."[48] In other words, the Greek understanding of being as οὐσία leaves an indelible mark on Western metaphysics such that all subsequent understandings of being have some relation to οὐσία as enduring presence.

While Plato's specific understanding of οὐσία is ἰδέα/εἶδος, Aristotle's specific understanding of οὐσία is ἐνέργεια [*energeia*], which Heidegger interprets as "worklike presence."[49] Heidegger states, "ἐνέργεια is perhaps the *most fundamental being-character* in Aristotle's doctrine of being. It contains the root word ἔργον [*ergon*]."[50] The Greek word ἔργον, from which the English word "ergonomics" is derived, means "work" and, therefore, according to Heidegger, "ἐνέργεια means 'standing in the work,' where 'work' means that which stands fully in its 'end.'"[51] Aristotle understands beings as always "on a work-like way" in that they are always functioning towards some end. For instance, the heart's end is the proper circulation of blood throughout the body, so we can say that the heart is "working well" when it is performing this function well. A heart that is not circulating the blood properly is not achieving its "end," or τέλος, and is therefore, in some sense, "less in being" from the Aristotelian perspective. For Aristotle, the heart is not an instantiation of the Form "heartness," as Plato would argue, and, thus, Aristotle's understanding of being is closer to the things themselves than Plato's; however, both Plato and Aristotle have gotten away from the pre-Socratic understanding of being as φύσις, since they establish a certain model of what it means to be in being rather than responding to the emerging into presence itself.

To recap, the initial understanding of being in the Greek world is φύσις, but this is—as Heidegger puts it—"immediately covered over"[52] by the Platonic and Aristotelian conceptions of οὐσία. For Plato, οὐσία is understood as ἰδέα/εἶδος, while for Aristotle οὐσία is understood as ἐνέργεια. Heidegger argues that the Platonic theory of the Forms, along with the Aristotelian notion of being as work-like presence or production, provides the intellectual scaffolding for the understanding of being that reigns in the medieval epoch.

THE MEDIEVAL EPOCH OF BEING

From a historical perspective, any understanding of the shift from ancient Greece to the Middle Ages or medieval times would be insufficient without an explanation of the rise and fall of the Roman Empire. Heidegger's history of being, however, is not historical in the sense of a chronicling of events. In *Being and Time*, Heidegger distinguishes between *Historie* and *Geschichte*.[53] While *Historie* is history from the historian's perspective, that is, from the perspective of the discipline of history, *Geschichte* is history from a philosophical perspective in that it examines the ontological orientations of Dasein. Heidegger's history of being, as *Seinsgeschichte*, examines the different worlds of Dasein in the various epochs. Nevertheless, some historical background in the sense of *Historie* may be helpful before engaging in *Geschichte*.

Historically, the Battle of Corinth of 146 B.C.E. is typically pointed to as a definitive marker in which the Romans began to overtake the Greeks as the center of the ancient Western world. Initially, the Roman world was similar to the Greek world in terms of philosophy and religion. Eventually, however, Christianity takes a hold in the Roman Empire, which incites a new epoch of being. While Jesus of Nazareth is the clear starting point of Christianity, since he is understood as the Christ or the Messiah, that is, the anointed one, Christianity as a religious movement begins with Saint Paul, who changes the meaning of παρουσία, which the Greeks abbreviated as οὐσία.[54] In a commentary on Saint Paul, Heidegger states, "In classical Greek παρουσία means arrival (presence). . . . For the Christian, however, παρουσία means 'the appearing again of the already appeared Messiah.' . . . With that . . . the entire structure of the concept is at once changed."[55] Indeed, a conversion to Christianity means one's entire world is transformed: "Paul shows: the gospel is strength for those who are called and it has the fundamental enactment of faith. Thus from out of this as fundamental experience, the entire factical life experience is determined, and all *significances* in it must be determined radically there-from."[56] Instead of regarding παρουσία/οὐσία as presence in general, παρουσία takes on the connotation of the presencing of the Messiah or Christ as God. This change in understanding is decisive in that it reorients what *matters* for Christians: what matters is the presencing of God, rather than the presence of worldly entities. Beings, for human beings in the medieval epoch, come to be seen as entirely contingent upon God's creation: "being is the creation of the creator. The supreme being (*summum ens*) is the Creator himself."[57] In the medieval world, God reorients the human understanding of what it is to *be*. The God of Christianity is the Creator, and natural entities come to be seen as *creatures of God*, which in Latin is *ens creatum.*

The break from the ancient Greek epoch of being to the medieval epoch is significant in that people from the different epochs live in different worlds; however, certain elements from the ancient Greek epoch provide bases for the Christian worldview. The Platonic duality between the supersensory realm of the Forms and the sensory world of particular beings sets up a ready hand distinction between heaven and earth that is crucial to Christianity. The realm of eternal Forms is swapped out for the eternal, heavenly realm of God, and the realm of the particular, sensory world is considered to be of less impor-tance than the eternal realm. This is why Heidegger agrees with Friedrich Nietzsche that "Christianity and its secularizations are generally 'Platonism for the people.'"[58] Aristotle also plays an important role in the transition from the ancient Greek to the medieval epoch. During the medieval period, Aris-totle comes to be seen simply as "*Ille Philosophus*"—the philosopher—by the medieval Scholastics, and the medieval understanding of being is linked with Aristotle's understanding of οὐσία as ἐνέργεια. As Zimmerman notes, "whereas for Aristotle ἐνέργεια continued to mean in part the self-manifesting or 'being' of an entity, for the Romans ἐνέργεια came to be understood not in ontological terms, but instead in terms of cause and effect: the 'action' involved in putting something together or manufacturing it."[59] Due to the Christian understanding of God being the almighty Creator of the world, all entities are *made* or *produced* by God in a causal fashion. Aristotle's under-standing of ἐνέργεια as work-like presence, such as the heart circulating the blood throughout the body, is not understood as having some necessary link to an almighty Creator. Rather, Aristotle has a sense of beings *as* self-produced. In the medieval period, the idea of beings as *produced* still holds, but the production comes to be understood through a Christian lens. Heidegger states, "In the medieval ontology the meaning of being . . . had been fixed by understanding it as an *ens creatum* [created being] . . . But createdness in the widest sense of something's having been produced, was an essential item in the structure of the ancient conception of being."[60]

In the medieval period, the answer to the question "What does it mean to be?" is answered: "to be created by God." Heidegger states, "the Christian conception of entities [is that of] *ens creatum*."[61] He continues, "Insofar as God as creator is the cause and the ground of all that is, the how, the way of asking [about what is], is oriented in advance towards this principle."[62] In other words, everything that *is* is understood from the lens of creation by the almighty Creator, God. Heidegger argues that this Christian way of understanding the world is less natural than the Greek way. He states, "The original nature that was disclosed . . . by the Greeks was later *de-natured* [*denaturiert*] . . . through Christianity, whereby nature was . . . depreciated to [the level of] 'the created.'"[63] The denaturing necessarily applies a restrictive theoretical lens on beings, making the interpretation of natural entities less "natural." God in the Christian world as the Creator is the ultimate causal agent, and this understanding of God infiltrates the Scholastic interpretation of Aristotle's philosophy. Heidegger states, "ἐνέργεια becomes *actualitas*,"[64] that which is actual. He continues, "*Actualitias*, however, is *causalitas*. The causal character of being as reality shows itself in all purity in that being which fulfills the essence of being in the highest sense, since it is that being which can never not be. Thought 'theologically,' this being is called 'God.'"[65] God, therefore, is the "most high" in that He is enduringly present as an eternal being, but also since he is the *cause* of everything that is *actual*.

To recap, from Heidegger's perspective, there is a degradation of the interpretation of natural entities as Western history unfolds. The original interpretation of being in ancient Greece, φύσις, which was degraded to παρουσία/ουσία by Plato and Aristotle, is taken to have a clear theological meaning of the presencing of Christ, that is, as God incarnate, for medieval people in the Western world. Given that God is the highest being, all beings—understood now as *actualitas*, that is, as that which is actual—are related to God causally in that He is the ultimate cause of their presence. The *causalitas/actualitas* understanding of reality provides the basis for a new understanding of being in the modern epoch initiated by René Descartes.

THE MODERN EPOCH OF BEING

Following the commonly held understanding of the history of Western philosophy, Heidegger points to Descartes as the founder of modern philosophy.

In fact, Heidegger states, "The whole of modern metaphysics taken together . . . maintains itself within the interpretation of what it is to be . . . that was prepared by Descartes."[66] Instead of viewing reality as ultimately being produced by God, persons in the modern epoch come to view reality as being represented by the modern subject. Our word "subject" is derived from the Greek word ὑποκείμενον [*hypokeimenon*], which Heidegger argues was understood as "everything that endures of itself and thus lies present [by the Greeks]."[67] As we pointed out earlier, the Greeks had an understanding of entities as beings that came to a stand of their own accord and endured in presence. Anything that does so is regarded as οὐσία and can be called a ὑποκείμενον if it has things predicated of it. When this term was translated into Latin during the medieval period, it was translated as *subiectum*. Heidegger states, "In the Middle Ages . . . *subiectum* . . . signified the ὑποκείμενον, that which lies present before us from out of itself, . . . whatever is present, e.g., things."[68] Of course, the specific understanding of the ὑποκείμενον of the Greeks and the *subiectum* of the medieval period has a different flavor. The Greeks see the ὑποκείμενον as having no inherent relation to any supernatural causal agent, while those living in the medieval period can only see the *subiectum* in terms of its relation to the Creator (e.g., the blossoming rose is now a blossoming rose *as created by God*). However, for both the Greeks and the people of medieval Europe, any entity that has things predicated of it can be referred to as a subject. Therefore, the subject has no special relation to the human being.

During the modern period initiated by Descartes, the notion of what it means to be a subject takes on an entirely new meaning in that only human selves are regarded as subjects. Heidegger states, "Until Descartes every thing present-at-hand for itself was a 'subject'; but now the 'I' becomes the special subject, that which regard to which all the remaining things first determine themselves as such. . . . The things themselves become 'objects.'"[69] Heidegger argues that Descartes designates the self or the "I" as the one and only subject, and all other things turn into objects. He states, "In Descartes' principle *ego cogito, ergo sum*, . . . man comes to be the self-posited ground and measure for all certitude and truth."[70] Descartes' famous statement, "*ego cogito, ergo sum*" ["I think, therefore, I am"], comes from his 1647 work, *Principles of Philosophy*. Here, he states, "I think, therefore I am, is the first and most certain [proposition] that occurs to one who philosophizes in an orderly way."[71] By making the existence of the self the most certain knowledge anyone could possibly have, Descartes gives the self unprecedented importance in the history of thought. According to Heidegger, the self becomes the one and only subject, and therefore underlies the knowledge of everything else, which is now understood as an aggregate of objects. Heidegger puts the point in the following way: "The certitude of the principle *cogito sum* determines the essence of all knowledge and everything knowable."[72] Everything outside the subject is now understood *in relation to* the subject. This initiates what is now commonly called Cartesian dualism in which there is a fundamental bifurcation of reality in terms of subjects and objects. Heidegger states, "The createdness of *ens creatum*, on the way that goes through Descartes has transformed itself into the objectness of absolute thinking . . . [This] is the Christian-Cartesian consolidation of οὐσία as ἰδέα in the absolute *I think of myself as the one who in such thinking intends things*."[73] Here, we can see the link between the various epochs of being quite clearly. The οὐσία as ἰδέα in Plato, coupled with the notion of *ens creatum* from the medieval epoch of being, provide the basis for Cartesian dualism wherein *ens creatum* has been bifurcated into two types: "the *res cogitans* and the *res extensa*."[74] The *res cogitans* is the "thinking being" or subject, while the *res extensa* are extended beings or objects.

We can call this shift in the understanding of what it means to be a subject and the coinciding introduction of the subject/object distinction "the Cartesian turn." This dualistic way of thinking was already prepared for in the medieval period with the distinction of Creator and created. Moreover, as Lynn White Jr. points out, there is already a sense that human beings are "special" in relation to other natural entities during the medieval period, since humans are seen as having a bond to the Creator that other beings simply do not have. In Genesis 1:26–27, humans are said to be created "in the image and likeness of God," and White points out that this means "man shares, in great measure, God's transcendence of nature."[75] In the Christian understanding, human beings are similar to all natural beings in that they are creatures of God, but they are also different from other natural beings in that they share God's image and likeness. One could say that humans are clearly *in nature*, but not entirely *of nature*. As God transcends His creation of nature and is therefore *super*-natural, humans can be said to transcend nature insofar as they are made in God's image and likeness, thereby occupying a position between the other entities of the natural world (plants, animals, etc.) and God Himself. One can see this clearly in Saint Augustine's *The City of God* in which he talks about the image of God that one can find in human beings, and how this makes humans nearer to God than anything else in all of natural creation.[76] Since the most essential aspect of human beings comes to be seen as their image and likeness to God, the idea that humans are supposed to turn away from their purely natural selves (e.g., their bodies, emotions, and instincts) and harbor their "supernatural" characteristics (e.g., their souls or rational minds) comes to take hold. In fact, the doctrine of a *contemptus mundi* [contempt for the world] became prevalent. Sean McDonagh notes, "The more mainstream Medieval spirituality . . . included a contempt for the world (*contemptus mundi*). . . . One finds it, for example, in many liturgical prayers. . . . Love for God was almost always seen in opposition to love for any creature."[77] Considering this, we can say that the beginnings of viewing oneself as essentially Other than the rest of nature can be found in the medieval period. Moreover, this bifurcation led to the idea that humans had to turn away from and even have contempt for the natural world and dedicate their lives to God in their quest to attain heavenly bliss.[78] In the Cartesian turn, the medieval idea that humans are exceptional in comparison to all other natural beings gets taken to a new level with the idea that humans are the one and only subjects.

Heidegger views the Cartesian turn as one of the most decisive events in all of Western metaphysics. He states, "Descartes' metaphysics is the decisive beginning of the foundation of metaphysics in the modern age."[79] In Cartesianism, the self is the only subject, and everything else is seen as an "object," which means "something thrown against you."[80] Heidegger states, "To the essence of object (*Gegenstand*) belongs the 'against' (*Gegen*) and the 'standing' (*Stand*)."[81] The German word for object, *Gegenstand*, which literally means "standing-against," shows us the true meaning of what it is to be an object. The key point here is that objects are not seen as things that come to a stand on their own accord. Rather, an object is in being *only insofar as it stands opposed to a subject.* Heidegger states, "The presence of the object shows itself in the representing, in which it becomes present *to me*."[82] The object gains its legitimacy as a being only by being opposed to a subject. While what was in being was understood in the sense of self-production in the Greek period and in the sense of God's production in the medieval period, it is now understood as what is produced by the subject in the modern period in the sense of what the subject represents.[83] The relationality of entities to the human being that we noted in the Greek notion of οὐσία has now been taken to an entirely new level. Indeed, Heidegger says explicitly that οὐσία as ἰδέα becomes "the correctness of apprehending and asserting"[84] of the subject.

Heidegger notes that the Cartesian turn has profound implications for how people in the modern period understand what it means to be. He states, "When man becomes the primary and only real *subiectum,* that means: Man becomes that being upon which all that is, is grounded as regards the manner of its being and its truth. *Man becomes the relational center of that which is as such*."[85] In other words, the designation of the self as the only subject makes the world a world *for me*. Everything that exists does so only insofar as I have conceived it. The blossoming rose is no longer seen as something that shines forth of its own accord or as something created by God; the blossoming rose is *as represented by me*. Since objects have no being of their own but are only in being insofar as they are presented to the subject, the world becomes a re-presentation of the subject. Thus, Heidegger states, "the world is changed into a doctrine of man"[86] in that "man founds and confirms himself as the authoritative measure for all standards of measure with which whatever can be accounted as certain—i.e., as true, i.e., as in being—is measured off and measured out."[87] To put it in a slightly different manner, we can say that the subject is able to choose the measure of what it means to be in being. For Descartes, this measure of truth is found in clear and distinct perception or intuition. In other words, Descartes' answer to the question "What is an entity?" is: "to be an object that has been clearly and distinctly perceived or intuited." In fact, one of Descartes' very first "rules of thought" as espoused in his *Rules for the Direction of the Mind* is as follows: "*We should concern ourselves only with those objects of which our minds appear to be adequate in gaining their certain and indubitable knowledge.*"[88]

Coming from a mathematical background, Descartes finds clear and distinct knowledge in that which can be quantified, and so clear and distinct knowledge of external objects lies in precisely measuring their quantifiable attributes in the Cartesian framework. In equating knowledge with the precise quantification of attributes, Descartes comes to see all objects in terms of their extension, and thus objects are considered to be *res extensa*. This universal understanding of objects can be seen in the following passage from Descartes: "I think that all bodies are made of one and the same matter, and there is nothing that makes any difference between them, except that the small parts of the matter that make up some shapes as distinct from others are arranged differently from those that make up the others."[89] Heidegger interprets this aspect of Descartes as follows: "Extension—namely, in length, breadth, and thickness—makes up the real being of that corporeal substance which we call 'world.'"[90] To be in being in the Cartesian framework, then, is to be an object in space and time with measurable properties of extension.

At this point we can see the defining difference between what it means to be in the modern epoch as compared to previous epochs. In previous epochs, a being was anything that endured in presence over time, whether understood on its own terms or from a Christian perspective. During the modern period, the emphasis is still on enduring presence, but this enduring presence is now seen in terms of what can be measured by the subject, which is extension. According to Heidegger, this emphasis on objective quantification provides the basis for all of modern science. Heidegger states, "what presences shows itself in the modern age in such a way as to bring its presencing to a stand in objectness. Science corresponds to this holding-sway of presencing in terms of objects."[91] Modern science accepts the basic Cartesian metaphysical framework of seeing the self as a subject that is attempting to gain clear and distinct knowledge of the objects of nature, which is seen as an aggregate of extended entities in space and time.

In precisely calculating the properties of objects, Heidegger notes that modern science focuses only on the aspects of the things that it has deemed important. In doing so, the understanding of nature comes to be a *representa-tion* of nature in accordance with the authoritative measures of science, rather than a glimpse into the nature of things themselves.[92] He states, "science always encounters only what *its* kind of representation has admitted before-hand as an object possible for science."[93] In viewing objects in nature from this restrictive theoretical lens, Heidegger says that our understanding of nature is "denatured" yet again. While the first denaturing of nature occurred when we began to view entities under the conceptual lens of being created by the Christian God in the medieval period, the second denaturing of nature happens "through modern natural science, which dissolved nature into the orbit of the mathematical order."[94]

During the first denaturing, humans are still seen as on a par with other natural beings insofar as they are created by God and are therefore included in the realm of *ens creatum*. While we pointed out that humans understand themselves as exceptional creatures due to their unique bond with the Creator, they understand themselves as creatures nonetheless. During this second denaturing, humans purport to sever themselves completely from nature by understanding themselves as the *distinctive* subjects and all other things as objects with calculable attributes. Heidegger notes that when nature is degraded to something that can be completely calculated by the subject, it is then understood as something that can be ordered to act in accordance with the subject's interests, which allows for the possibility of exploitation.[95] When the world becomes a world *for me*, as a subject, I have a greater likelihood to only emphasize the aspects of entities that are directly relevant to my own being and my self-interests. Guignon puts the point in the following way: "When the subject is interpreted as the ground of all beings, being comes to be understood as something merely at man's disposal. Nature and the world are regarded as something on hand for fulfilling our utilitarian ends."[96] During the first dena-turing, humans could still view entities as God's creation and potentially respect them as such; however, when nature is viewed as something essentially separate from human beings as subjects, and therefore as something *essentially Other*, the possibility of exploitation grows tremendously.

One can find the roots of the possibility of exploitation already in the thought of Descartes. In his *Discourse on Method*, he states that his hope is:

> to find a practical philosophy, by means of which, knowing the force and the actions of fire, water, air, the stars, the heavens, and all the other bodies that surround us, just as distinctly as we know the various skills of our craftsmen, we might be able, in the same way, to use them for all the purposes for which they are appropriate, and thus render ourselves, as it were, *masters and possessors of nature* . . . [This] would enable one to enjoy trouble-free the fruits of the earth and all the goods found there.[97]

Here, we can see that Descartes does not simply seek clear and distinct knowledge of nature for knowledge's sake; rather, a correlative goal is to master nature and utilize the earth's "bounty" for our human interests. At the same time, however, Descartes is humble enough to realize that natural beings are not to be viewed strictly in terms of their resourcefulness to humans. As a thinker still ensconced in the late medieval period (yet simultaneously initiating a new period), Descartes himself believes in God as the Creator of nature, and does not believe that God created the world simply so that humans can be masters and possessors of it. In fact, he calls such a belief "childish and absurd": "It would be childish and absurd for a metaphysician to assert that God, like some vainglorious human being, had no other purpose in making the universe than to win men's praise; or that the sun, which is many times larger than the earth, was created for no other purpose than to give light to man, who occupies a very small part of the earth."[98] While the historical Descartes is not to blame for the idea that nature is merely there to be mastered, his thought helps to set the seed that knowledge of nature is related to control of nature.

As the modern period continues and scientists come to gain an increasing understanding of nature as an aggregate of calculable objects, the idea that humans are able to master or control nature takes a firm hold. This is precisely what the modern philosopher and (meta)scientist[99] Sir Francis Bacon meant when he penned the oft-quoted saying that "knowledge is power."[100] Bacon, who was an approximate contemporary of Descartes, says that the modern sciences do not "merely exert a gentle guidance over nature's course; they have the power to conquer and subdue her, to shake her to her foundations."[101] As David Oldroyd points out in his commentary on Bacon, "Man is to try to 'command' nature, and wrest her secrets from her, thereby producing fruits for the benefit of mankind. It is this injunction that Western man has followed so successfully yet also with such potentially disastrous results."[102] The emphasis in modern science is not merely in understanding the world and attaining knowledge; *it is on attaining knowledge that allows us to master nature.* This can only make sense under the Cartesian framework in which humans are seen as subjects, and nature is seen as objects set against the subjects that not only interpret them but also manipulate them. The self becomes separate from the rest of nature, and its goal is to understand and conquer this opposing realm.

We should point out at the outset that there is something clearly right about viewing nature in terms of quantifiable entities in space and time. This is not only a useful way in which to approach entities from a scientific perspective, it has also allowed us to make undeniable progress in the Western world. The modern period has not only allowed for developments in the scientific fields of medicine, physics, chemistry, et cetera, but also provided the foundation for the Industrial Revolution and the various technological advances we have seen in the past three and a half centuries. People live longer, healthier, and flat-out better lives due to the advances in the sciences. At the same time, however, it is this very success that has led us to believe that this is the *only* way in which to understand reality, and this is where the problem lies. In other words, the scientific, industrial, and technological developments that are based on Cartesian metaphysics have been so successful that we have come to view reality strictly in the Cartesian way. Heidegger understands the successes that modern science and technology have championed, but also notes that "the technological-scientific rationalization ruling in the present age justifies itself every day more surprisingly by its immense results."[103] Along with the successes comes the ever-expanding entrenchment of the Cartesian understanding of reality. We see the subject/object model to be the only way in which reality should be understood, and we see nature as the aggregate of objects in space and time as the only way in which to see it. The problem here is that the modern scientific conception of nature becomes "the only game in town," so to speak, and other potentially viable conceptions of nature are no longer taken seriously. In fact, in assuming that the modern conception of nature is the right one, all other possible ways of viewing the nature of reality come to lose legitimacy.

The view that science is the only legitimate picture of reality has come to be called "scientism." Heidegger points out the problems with scientism in his 1954 essay, "Science and Reflection." As science gains an increasing amount of success, the methods of science are adopted in an increasing amount of areas of the Western world. Heidegger points out that the proliferation of the power of science does not only mean that we now see reality in the specifically Cartesian way, but we also accept the Cartesian-*cum*-scientific methodology. In an earlier work, Heidegger states, "'Method' is now the name for the securing, conquering proceeding against beings, in order to capture them as objects for the subject."[104] We now find scientific methodologies employed in disciplines as far ranging as communication, sociology, psychology, history, philosophy, and even art. In seeing the pervasiveness of the power of science, Heidegger argued that "science has developed such a power as could never have been met with on earth before, and . . . consequently this power is ultimately to be spread over the entire globe."[105] As the power of science increases, it comes to be seen as the only legitimate source of truth and knowledge, and its metaphysical underpinnings soon become entrenched in various areas. So the success of science not only makes us accept science as an authority when it comes to truth and knowledge, but it also turns us all into Cartesians, whether we know it or not and whether we like it or not.

Heidegger points to Max Planck's well-known statement "That is real which can be measured" as a fitting statement of scientism. In his commentary on this statement, Heidegger says "the decision about what may pass in science . . . for assured knowledge rests with the measurability supplied in the objectness of nature and, in keeping with that measurability, *in the possibilities inherent in the measuring procedure.*"[106] If we couple this with the scientistic idea that "*science is the theory of the real,*"[107] we come to find that our understanding of reality is only as rich and diverse as what science deems worthy of being measured. And since the only things that science deems worthy of measurement are whatever can be clearly and distinctly calculated, reality comes to be seen as "a coherence of motion of material bodies"[108] and nothing else.

Even if it were the case that science could come upon a perfect theory of nature and map the coordinates and motions of all material bodies and be able to precisely predict their future movements (as, say, God the Creator and ultimate causal agent could do given his creation of *actualitas* in the medieval period), this would still only be one way of looking at nature. As Heidegger states, "Theory never outstrips nature. . . . Scientific representation is never able to encompass the coming to presence of nature; for the objectness of nature is, antecedently, only *one* way in which nature exhibits itself . . . The representing and securing [of modern science can never be] able to encompass the essential fullness of nature."[109] Indeed, the very fact that we have experienced different epochs of being in the history of metaphysics shows that nature is not necessarily to be understood merely as a coherence of calculable objects. Not only are there different ways of understanding nature, we will follow Heidegger in believing that there may be more appropriate ways in which to understand nature.

Before we attempt to see what a more appropriate revealing of nature may look like, however, we have to understand how it comes about that nature comes to be seen as standing-reserve in the latter parts of the modern period. In the mid-1930s, Heidegger offers this prophetic statement: "[The] gigantic progress of sciences in the future . . . will bring exploitation and usage of the earth . . . that are still inconceivable today."[110] Heidegger saw the seeds of environmental exploitation in the progress of the sciences and technological advances long before we came upon the current environmental crises of anthropogenic climate change and resource depletions in the Anthropocene. Instead of repudiating modern science and the scientific, industrial, and technological progress accompanying it, Heidegger tried to understand how the changes brought about by the scientific, industrial, and technological progress eventually brought about a new way of revealing entities in what he calls the age of modern technology. Here, objects are no longer seen as things that stand against the subject, since they have become completely calculable and interchangeable units of energy and are thereby merely seen as undifferentiated material on hand to be exploited. This initiates the "unrestrained exploitation of the earth" that we spoke of in chapter 1, which culminates in the environmental crisis. Heidegger argues that the modern physical theory of nature grounded in Cartesian metaphysics leads to the current age of modern technology. He states, "The modern physical theory of nature prepares the way first not simply for technology but for the essence of modern technology [wherein everything is viewed as standing-reserve]. For already in physics the challenging gathering-together into ordering revealing holds sway."[111] It will be our task in the next chapter to see how the modern epoch of being culminates in the current age of modern technology and how this relates to our environmental crisis.

NOTES

1. Charles Guignon notes that the term "history of being" takes on different meanings for Heidegger throughout his works in his essay, "The History of Being," in *A Companion to Heidegger*, ed. Hubert Dreyfus and Mark Wrathall (Malden, Mass.: Blackwell, 2005), 392–406. For our purposes, we can understand the history of being in the most basic sense of the various epochal understandings of being in Western metaphysics.

2. Heidegger, "Overcoming Metaphysics," in *The End of Philosophy*, trans. Joan Stambaugh (Chicago: The University of Chicago Press, 2003), 86 [GA 7, 70].

3. Heidegger, "Overcoming Metaphysics," 90 [GA 7, 75].

4. Guignon, "Introduction," 17.

5. Iain Thomson notes that Heidegger's mature history of being delineates five basic epochs (the pre-Socratic, Platonic, medieval, modern, and late-modern) in *Heidegger on Ontotheology: Technology and the Politics of Education* (Cambridge: Cambridge University Press, 2005), 25. For our purposes, splitting up the history of being into three epochs is sufficient.

6. Heidegger, *Being and Time*, 93 [GA 2, 87].

7. Hubert L. Dreyfus, *Being-in-the-World: A Commentary on Heidegger's Being and Time, Division I* (Cambridge and London: The MIT Press, 1991), 89–90.

8. Thomas E. Wartenberg, "Heidegger," in *The Routledge Companion to Aesthetics*, second edition, ed. Berys Gaut and McIver Lopes (New York: Routledge, 2001), 154.

9. Heidegger, *The Principle of Reason*, 91 [GA 10, 135].

10. Heidegger, *Introduction to Metaphysics*, 15 [GA 40, 10].

11. Liddell and Scott's *Greek-English Lexicon* translates φύσις as "*the nature, natural qualities, powers, constitution*, of a person or thing," 876 (emphasis in original).

12. Heidegger, *Introduction to Metaphysics*, 18 [GA 40, 12].

13. Heidegger, *Introduction to Metaphysics*, 15–16 [GA 40, 11].

14. Cf. Heidegger, *Contributions to Philosophy*, 155 [GA 65, 222].

15. Martin Heidegger, "The Anaximander Fragment," in *Early Greek Thinking: The Dawn of Western Philosophy*, trans. David Farrell Krell and Frank A. Capuzzi (San Francisco: Harper & Row, 1975), 39 [GA 5, 352].

16. Cf. Heidegger, "The Anaximander Fragment," 50 [GA 5, 364].

17. Heidegger equates being with "the very presencing of what is present" in "Logos (Heraclitus, Fragment B 50)," in *Early Greek Thinking: The Dawn of Western Philosophy*, trans. David Farrell Krell and Frank A. Capuzzi (San Francisco: Harper & Row, 1975), 64 [GA 7, 218].

18. Cf. the translators' footnote in *Being and Time*, 22.

19. Heidegger, *The Principle of Reason*, 125 [GA 10, 146] (emphasis added).

20. Richard Polt, *The Emergency of Being: On Heidegger's* Contributions to Philosophy (Ithaca and London: Cornell University Press, 2006), 58.

21. Heidegger, *Being and Time*, 29 [GA 2, 12].

22. Martin Heidegger, *The Basic Problems of Phenomenology*, 78 [GA 24, 109]. We should point out that in his later thought, Heidegger begins to try to think of being as it is in itself with his notion of *Seyn* (be-ing), thereby severing this interdependence of being and beings. In *Contributions to Philosophy*, for instance, he states, "be-ing can no longer be thought of in the perspective of beings; it must be enthought from within be-ing *itself*" (5 [GA 65, 7]).

23. Heidegger, *Introduction to Metaphysics*, 226 [GA 40, 154].

24. Heidegger, *Contributions to Philosophy*, 8 [GA 65, 10].

25. Martin Heidegger, *Nietzsche, Volume III: The Will to Power as Knowledge and as Metaphysics*, ed. David Farrell Krell (New York: Harper & Row, 1987), 250 [GA 6.2, 333].

26. Heidegger, "The Anaximander Fragment," 57 [GA 5, 372].

27. Martin Heidegger, *What Is Called Thinking?* trans. Fred D. Wieck and J. Glenn Gray (New York: Harper & Row, 1968), 92 [GA 8, 96]. Heidegger also says, " 'In being' means: being present. Beings are more in being the more present they are. Beings come to be more present, the more abidingly they abide, the more lasting the abiding is" (*What Is Called Thinking?* 101 [GA 8, 104]). Here we can see clearly the emphasis on enduring presence.

28. Cf. Martin Heidegger, *Pathmarks*, 200 [GA 9, 260].

29. Martin Heidegger, "Metaphysics as History of Being," in *The End of Philosophy*, trans. Joan Stambaugh (Chicago: The University of Chicago Press, 1973), 28 [GA 6.2, 431].

30. Heidegger, *Introduction to Metaphysics*, 70 [GA 40, 48].

31. Liddell and Scott translate οὐσία as "*that which is one's own, one's substance, property*" and "*the being, essence, nature* of a thing" (*Greek-English Lexicon*, 579; emphasis in original).

32. Heidegger, *Introduction to Metaphysics*, 215 [GA 40, 147].

33. Heidegger, *Introduction to Metaphysics*, 200 [GA 40, 137].

34. Heidegger, *Introduction to Metaphysics*, 202 [GA 40, 138].

35. Plato's Allegory of the Cave is the most famous passage on the Forms. See Plato, *Republic*, trans. G. M. A. Grube and C. D. C. Reeve (Indianapolis/Cambridge: Hackett, 1992), Book VII.

36. Heidegger, *Nietzsche, Volume III*, 59 [GA 47, 114].

37. Heidegger, *Nietzsche, Volume III*, 58 [GA 47, 114].

38. Cf. Martin Heidegger, "Metaphysics as History of Being," 9 [GA 6.2, 409].

39. Martin Heidegger, *Basic Concepts of Aristotelian Philosophy*, trans. Robert D. Metcalf and Mark B. Tanzer (Bloomington and Indianapolis: Indiana University Press, 2009), 154 [GA 18, 229].

40. Cf. Martin Heidegger, "Metaphysics as History of Being," 10 [GA 6.2, 409].

41. Heidegger, *Pathmarks*, 229 [GA 9, 300].

42. Cf. Heidegger, *Pathmarks*, 203 [GA 9, 266].

43. Cf. Heidegger, "The Anaximander Fragment," 15 [GA 5, 324].

44. Heidegger, *Basic Concepts of Aristotelian Philosophy*, 19 [GA 18, 25].

45. Heidegger, *Basic Concepts of Aristotelian Philosophy*, 18 [GA 18, 24].

46. Heidegger, *Basic Concepts of Aristotelian Philosophy*, 18 [GA 18, 24].

47. Heidegger, *Basic Concepts of Aristotelian Philosophy*, 25 [GA 18, 33].

48. Heidegger, *Contributions to Philosophy*, 317 [GA 65, 450].

49. Heidegger, "Metaphysics as History of Being," 19. Heidegger also focuses in on Aristotle's notion of ἐντελέχεια [*entelecheia*] as Aristotle's basic understanding of being. Cf. *Mindfulness*, 351 [GA 66, 397].

50. Heidegger, *Basic Concepts of Aristotelian Philosophy*, 31 [GA 18, 42].

51. Heidegger, *Pathmarks*, 217 [GA 9, 284].

52. Heidegger, *Contributions to Philosophy*, 155 [GA 65, 222].

53. Cf. *Being and Time*, 30, footnote 1.

54. Χριστός [*Christos*] is the Greek translation of the Hebrew "Messiah." Cf. *Greek-English Lexicon*, 895.

55. Martin Heidegger, *The Phenomenology of Religious Life*, trans. Matthias Fritsch and Jennifer Anna Gosetti-Ferencei (Bloomington and Indianapolis: Indiana University Press, 2004), 71 [GA 60, 102].

56. Heidegger, *The Phenomenology of Religious Life*, 97 [GA 60, 137].

57. Heidegger, *Nietzsche, Volume III*, 226 [GA 6.2, 302].

58. Heidegger, *Contributions to Philosophy*, 153 [GA 65, 219]. Cf. Friedrich Nietzsche, *Beyond Good and Evil: Prelude to a Philosophy of the Future*, trans. Walter Kaufmann (New York: Vintage, 1989), 2.

59. Zimmerman, *Heidegger's Confrontation with Modernity*, 170.

60. Heidegger, *Being and Time*, 46 [GA 2, 33].

61. Heidegger, *What Is a Thing?* trans. W. B. Barton Jr. and Vera Deutsch (Chicago: Henry Regnery Company, 1967), 110 [GA 41, 110].

62. Heidegger, *What Is a Thing?* 110 [GA 41, 110].

63. Heidegger, GA 39, 195.

64. Heidegger, "Metaphysics as History of Being," 11 [GA 6.2, 410].

65. Heidegger, "Metaphysics as History of Being," 15 [GA 6.2, 415].

66. Martin Heidegger, "The Age of the World Picture," 127 [GA 5, 88].

67. Heidegger, "Metaphysics as History of Being," 28 [GA 6.2, 431].

68. Heidegger, *Pathmarks*, 57–58 [GA 9, 63].

69. Heidegger, *What Is a Thing?* 105 [GA 41, 106]. Heidegger defines a thing in the sense of being present-at-hand as any animate or inanimate thing (cf. *What Is a Thing?* 6 [GA 41, 6]).

70. Martin Heidegger, *Nietzsche, Volume IV: Nihilism*, ed. David Farrell Krell (New York: HarperCollins, 1991), 90 [GA 6.2, 134].

71. René Descartes, *Principles of Philosophy*, in *René Descartes: Philosophical Essays and Correspondence*, ed. Roger Ariew (Indianapolis: Hackett Publishing Company, 2000), 232.

72. Heidegger, *Nietzsche, Volume IV*, 116 [GA 6.2, 164].

73. Heidegger, *Mindfulness*, 251 [GA 66, 283–284].

74. Heidegger, *Being and Time*, 126 [GA 2, 124].

75. Lynn White Jr., "The Historical Roots of Our Ecological Crisis," *Science* 155, no. 3767 (1967): 1205.

76. Cf. Saint Augustine, *Concerning The City of God against the Pagans*, trans. Henry Bettenson (London and New York: Penguin, 1984), 459. If consulting other translations, see Book XI, chapter 26.

77. Sean McDonagh, *The Greening of the Church* (London: G. Chapman Publishers, 1990), 19–20.

78. Heidegger shows how this is related to Plato's Forms in his "Letter on 'Humanism'": "The Christian sees the *humanitas* of *homo*, in contradistinction to *Deitas*. He is the human being of the history of redemption who as a 'child of God' hears and accepts the call of the Father in Christ. The human being is not of this world, since the 'world,' thought in terms of Platonic theory, is only a temporary passage to the beyond" (*Pathmarks*, 244 [GA 9, 319]).

79. Heidegger, *Nietzsche, Volume IV*, 100 [GA 6.2, 147].

80. Heidegger, *What Is a Thing?* 26 [GA 41, 25].

81. Heidegger, *What Is a Thing?* 184 [GA 41, 188].

82. Heidegger, *What Is a Thing?* 188 [GA 41, 192].

83. It will be useful to make a distinction between Descartes' own philosophy and Cartesianism, which is the understanding of reality strictly in terms of subjects and objects. While in the Cartesian framework that eventually wins out there are only subjects and objects, Descartes' own ontology includes the cognizing subject, objects, and the Christian God. The Cartesian framework that I will reference is the understanding of the world strictly in terms of subjects and objects.

84. Heidegger, *Pathmarks*, 177 [GA 9, 231].

85. Heidegger, "The Age of the World Picture," 128 [GA 5, 88] (emphasis added).

86. Heidegger, "The Age of the World Picture," 133 [GA 5, 93].

87. Heidegger, "The Age of the World Picture," 151 [GA 5, 110].

88. René Descartes, *Rules for the Direction of the Mind*, in *René Descartes: Philosophical Essays and Correspondence*, ed. Roger Ariew (Indianapolis: Hackett Publishing Company, 2000), 3 (emphasis in original).

89. René Descartes, "To the Marquis of Newcastle," in *René Descartes: Philosophical Essays and Correspondence*, ed. Roger Ariew (Indianapolis: Hackett Publishing Company, 2000), 275.

90. Heidegger, *Being and Time*, 123 [GA 2, 121].

91. Martin Heidegger, "Science and Reflection," in *The Question Concerning Technology and Other Essays*, trans. William Lovitt (New York: Harper & Row, 1977), 167 [GA 7, 49–50].

92. Heidegger himself does not think that we can ever see being as it is in itself, since he does not think that there is a "view from nowhere" but rather sees all comprehension as perspectival. However, as we will see in chapter 4, he does think that

there are alternative ways of understanding entities in distinction from the ones that one finds in modern science, and these ways are often more appropriate than the ones that come forth from the scientific perspective (in certain contexts).

93. Martin Heidegger, "The Thing," in *Poetry, Language, Thought*, trans. Albert Hofstadter (Harper & Row: New York, 1971), 170 [GA 7, 171].

94. Heidegger, GA 39, 195.

95. Cf. Heidegger, *Contributions to Philosophy*, 63 [GA 65, 91].

96. Charles B. Guignon, *Heidegger and the Problem of Knowledge* (Indianapolis: Hackett Publishing Company, 1983), 19.

97. René Descartes, *Discourse on Method*, in *René Descartes: Philosophical Essays and Correspondence*, ed. Roger Ariew (Indianapolis: Hackett Publishing Company, 2000), 74 (my emphasis).

98. René Descartes, "To Hyperaspistes, August 1641," in *The Philosophical Writings of Descartes, Volume III: The Correspondence*, trans. John Cottingham et al. (Cambridge: Cambridge University Press, 1991), 195.

99. As most historians point out when discussing Francis Bacon, he himself was not much of a scientist, since he did not make any significant scientific discoveries. Nevertheless, Bacon's emphasis on how a systematic understanding of nature will lead to a control of nature was extremely influential to modern scientific institutions, especially in regard to the idea that there needs to be a coherent scientific method. Those interested in this connection should consult William T. Lynch's "A Society of Baconians? The Collective Development of Bacon's Method in the Royal Society of London," in *Francis Bacon and the Refiguring of Early Modern Thought*, ed. Julie Robin Solomon and Catherine Gimelli Martin (Hants, England and Burlington, Vt.: Ashgate, 2005).

100. Cf. Francis Bacon, *Meditations Sacræ*, in *Meditations Sacræ and Human Philosophy* (Whitefish, Mont.: Kessinger Publishing, 1996), 32.

101. Francis Bacon, *The Philosophy of Francis Bacon*, trans. Benjamin Farrington (Chicago: University of Chicago Press, 1964), 93.

102. David Oldroyd, *The Arch of Knowledge: An Introductory Study of the History of the Philosophy and Methodology of Science* (New York and London: Methuen, 1986), 60.

103. Martin Heidegger, "The End of Philosophy and the Task of Thinking," in *Basic Writings*, revised and expanded edition, ed. David Farrell Krell (New York: HarperCollins, 1993), 448 [GA 14, 88].

104. Heidegger, *Nietzsche, Volume IV*, 120 [GA 6.2, 170]. In "The Age of the World Picture," Heidegger says something similar in stating that "the real system of science consists in a solidarity of procedure and attitude with respect to the objectification of whatever is" (126 [GA 5, 86]).

105. Heidegger, "Science and Reflection," 156 [GA 7, 39].

106. Heidegger, "Science and Reflection," 169 [GA 7, 52] (my emphasis).

107. Heidegger, "Science and Reflection," 157 [GA 7, 40].

108. Heidegger, "Science and Reflection," 171 [GA 7, 53].

109. Heidegger, "Science and Reflection," 173–174 [GA 7, 55–56].

110. Heidegger, *Contributions to Philosophy*, 108 [GA 65, 156–157].

111. Heidegger, "The Question Concerning Technology," 22 [GA 7, 23].

Chapter Three

The Contemporary Period

In the modern period, all entities come to be seen as objects that stand against the subject whose goal is to attain clear and distinct knowledge of objects. Moreover, since it is the subject who gets to decide the criteria for what counts as clear and distinct knowledge, the subject decides which aspects of the objects are most important and therefore most relevant. In the Cartesian framework that eventually wins out, the crucial aspects of objects are those that can be clearly and distinctly perceived, which ends up being qualities of extension, since such qualities can be precisely quantified. We noted in the previous chapter that Descartes changes the understanding of the *being* of entities by specifying extension to be the definitive aspect of objects. In the modern period, a being is no longer understood as an entity that endures in presence and stands on its own, as it did in the ancient Greek epoch, or a creation of the great Creator, the Christian God, as it did in the medieval period. Rather, what it means to be a being in the modern period is to be an object with quantifiable extended attributes opposed to a subject. We have also pointed out that Cartesian metaphysics provides the ground for modern science. Our task in this chapter is to get a better idea as to how modern science differs from previous science in the Western world, how the modern period culminates in the age of modern technology wherein everything is seen as an undifferentiated grid of resources on hand for human consumption, and how this aligns with our current environmental crisis.

THE MATHEMATICAL IN MODERN SCIENCE

We noted in chapter 2 how heavily Aristotle influenced the medieval intellectuals. This was especially true in their analysis of the natural world.[1]

39

Considering this, for our purposes, we can say that medieval science was essentially Aristotelian.[2] During the time of Descartes, Aristotelian science began to fall out of favor among some intellectuals who sought a new way of going about doing science. Historian of science Herbert Butterfield notes, "Attacks on Aristotle had been increasingly common and sometimes exceedingly bitter in the sixteenth century."[3] He points to Bacon and Descartes as the eventual leaders of the movement to initiate a science that was not Aristotelian. The question that is most relevant for us is what makes modern science so distinctive and unprecedented in the history of Western thought, which will then allow us to see the connection between modern science and the age of modern technology. The answer that is commonly given is that modern science emphasized a new method that went beyond anything that could be found in ancient or medieval thought. Butterfield notes that this was precisely Bacon's view: "Now it was Bacon's firm principle that if men wanted to achieve anything new in the world, it was of no use attempting to reach it on any ancient method—they must realize that new practices and policies would be necessary. He stressed above all the need for the direction of experiments—an end to the mere haphazard experimenting."[4] In the first few pages of Bacon's *New Organum*, a work written as an affront to Aristotle's *Organum*, Bacon attempts to demonstrate the illegitimacy of the old sciences and establish a new scientific method, which he calls a new organum. He states unabashedly, "the sciences we now have are no more than elegant arrangements of things previously discovered, not methods of discovery or pointers to new results."[5] He goes on to say that "a more certain and altogether better intellectual procedure must come into use."[6] Here, Bacon is explicitly calling for a revolutionary way in which to go about doing science.

Descartes, in contrast, is much subtler than Bacon. Instead of calling for a new method of going about scientific inquiry by explicitly attacking Aristotelianism, he engages in a subterfuge tactic in his *Meditations* in which he tries to get Aristotelians to become Cartesians without them knowing that they are actually giving up Aristotelianism in doing so. In a letter to his friend and fellow philosopher Marin Mersenne, he states:

> I will tell you, between us, that these six meditations contain all the foundations of my physics. But it will not do to say this, if you please; for those who favor Aristotle would perhaps find it more difficult to approve of them. And I hope that those who read them will accustom themselves insensibly to my principles, and will recognize the truth before noticing that they destroy those of Aristotle.[7]

Here, we can see that Descartes is opposing Aristotelian science, though his tactic is different than Bacon's since he attempts to implement his physics and methodology covertly. Regardless of the ways in which to bring about a change, it is clear not only that a shift occurred during the early modern period when it comes to science, but also that the leaders of the movement knew that they were revolutionizing the way in which to do science.

Historians of science often point to a new sort of method or technique grounded in mathematics adopted by early modern intellectuals that brought about the shift from Aristotelian science to modern science. Consider, for instance, this excerpt from Lawrence Principe's *The Scientific Revolution*: "The technique of reducing the physical world into mathematical abstractions, and eventually into formulas and algorithms, championed by Galileo, played a key role in producing a new physics, and stands as a distinctive feature of the Scientific Revolution [during the early modern period]."[8] Principe argues that the major shift that occurred was a shift in methodology that emphasizes mathematical abstraction. Heidegger agrees that a fundamental root of modern thought lies in the unprecedented emphasis on the mathematical in both the sciences and philosophy. He states, "Modern natural science [and] modern metaphysics sprang from the same root of the mathematical in the wider sense."[9] Here, one might think that Heidegger would agree with Principe in saying that what is distinctive about the modern period is its use of mathematical abstraction in utilizing tools like algorithms or formulas since, when we think of the mathematical today, we often think exclusively in these terms. However, while we tend to equate the mathematical with algorithms, formulas, or the numerical as such, Heidegger shows that the mathematical is wider than the numerical: "We are long used to thinking of numbers when we think of the mathematical. The mathematical and numbers are obviously connected. Only the question remains: Is this connection because the mathematical is numerical in character, or, on the contrary, is the numerical something mathematical? The second is the case."[10] Heidegger points to the roots of the word "mathematics," which comes from the Greek word μαθήματα [*mathemata*] to make his case: "the μαθήματα are the things insofar as we take cognizance of them as what we already know them to be in advance."[11] The mathematical in this wider sense, then, is that which can be known in advance, which can be juxtaposed with the mathematical in the narrow sense that deals specifically with numbers. It is the emphasis on the mathematical in the wider sense that makes modern science different than its predecessors in Western thought, not simply the fact that the modern sciences utilize numerical quantification, algorithms, or formulas to bolster their findings. Both Descartes and Bacon seek for a clear-cut, *universal* method of going about inquiry of the natural world, and this way of having a plan of going about inquiry *in advance* is in line with the mathematical in the wider sense.

Heidegger notes that the wider sense of the mathematical was important during the ancient Greek period. For instance, he points to Plato's motto at the entrance of the Academy: "Ἀγεωμέτρητος μηδεὶς εἰσίτω [*Ageometretos medeis eisito*]," which he translates as "Let no one who has not grasped the mathematical enter here!"[12] However, the mathematical comes to gain unprecedented prominence in the thought of Descartes, who urges that "we reject all knowledge that is only probable, and we declare that only those things ought to be believed which are *perfectly known and of which there can be no doubt.*"[13] In order to focus explicitly on knowledge that can be perfectly known, Descartes gives the mathematical as μαθήματα preeminent importance. In speaking of Descartes, Heidegger states, "the mathematical . . . expressly intends to explicate itself as the standard of *all* thought and to establish the rules which thereby arise."[14] He continues, "Descartes . . . posits the mathematical as the absolute ground and seeks for all knowledge a foundation that will be in accord with it."[15] In seeking absolute certainty of objects, Descartes focuses explicitly and exclusively on the aspects of things that can be known in advance, that is, their extended qualities. Anything that does not fall into the rubric of the mathematical is simply ignored as probable, and is therefore not considered to be a genuine candidate of knowledge.

Heidegger states that "the modern concept of science" can be found in the thought of Descartes.[16] As the modern sciences adopt Cartesian metaphysics and the Cartesian method, they also adopt Descartes' emphasis on the mathematical and therefore focus only on the aspects of things that can be known in advance. For the modern sciences, nature comes to be seen as a configuration of bodies that can be decisively known through calculation.[17] But, as Heidegger notes, this decisive knowledge is only possible because modern science has already stipulated which aspects of entities are important and has closed off anything that cannot be quantified with precision in advance. The result is that the world turns into a representation of the interests of modern science. Just as the natural world of Descartes is the world as *represented to the knowing subject*, the natural world of modern science is the world as already conceived by the modern scientist, which is a coherence of extended, quantifiable bodies in motion that can be known in advance via the use of the scientific methods.

Although we have seen that the mathematical in the sense of μαθήματα was considered important during the ancient Greek epoch, this overarching emphasis on the mathematical cannot be found in the Aristotelian science that reigned in the ancient and medieval periods. As Heidegger points out, Aristotle's goal was "to say that which corresponds to what shows itself."[18] Aristotle attempts to find the inner principle that guides each particular entity in its movements, and we can call this inner principle its *nature*. In Aristotelian science, one finds different natures in different entities, as Heidegger explains: "The body moves according to its nature . . . The purely earthly body moves downward, the purely fiery body—as every blazing flame demonstrates—moves upward. Why? Because the earthly has its place below, the fiery, above. Each body has *its* place *according to its kind*, and it strives toward that place."[19] As we noted in chapter 2, Aristotle understands beings as having a certain ἐνέργεια that strives toward a τέλος. In Aristotelian science, natural bodies seek different places according to their particular natures, and the scientist's goal is to understand the nature of these inner principles that guide natural bodies. This is the basic understanding of the way in which entities work in the ancient period. Moreover, Aristotle's understanding of natural bodies was "taken over by the medieval Scholastics,"[20] and scientists in the medieval period agree with Aristotle that natural bodies have their own guiding inner principles, though these principles were both created and implanted by God since they are *ens creatum*.[21] In the modern conception, the idea that different natural bodies have different natures no longer holds because all of nature comes to be seen as a coherence of bodies in motion.[22]

In accepting the Cartesian-*cum*-Baconian scientific methodology and the emphasis on the mathematical, the modern scientist focuses only on the aspects of objects that can be quantitatively measured and, in doing so, already stipulates a conception of nature in accordance with the interests of modern science.[23] Heidegger explains the result of this stipulation as follows: "We feel that what zoology and botany investigate concerning animals and plants and how they investigate it may be correct. But are they still animals and plants? *Are they not machines duly prepared beforehand?*"[24] Here, Heidegger is stressing that the modern scientist already brings along his or her conception of what it means *to be* in attempting to understand the natural world and, in doing so, does not respect the entities on their own terms. In other words, instead of heeding the Aristotelian creed of "saying that which corresponds to what shows itself," the modern scientist stipulates in advance what sorts of qualities of objects are worthy of examination. In doing so, we can say that scientists in the modern period operate within a preset, inherently limited realm of scientific inquiry, since only that which can be precisely quantitatively measured is available for inquiry.

Heidegger points out that this emphasis on the mathematical permeates all of modern science, and since modern science also gained the legacy of Descartes' emphasis on certainty, modern science becomes the activity of gaining exact knowledge of the objects of nature in order to attain certainty. He states, "The rigor of the mathematical physical science is exactitude. Here all events, *if they are to enter at all into representation as events of nature*, must be defined beforehand as spatiotemporal magnitudes of motion. Such defining is accomplished through measuring, with the help of number and calculation."[25] As we pointed out in the previous chapter, this emphasis on exactitude is not only important because scientists strive to "get things right" and therefore be certain of our knowledge of nature. Rather, the idea is also that if we can successfully map out the coordinates of the motions of the objects of nature, we

[handwritten margin note: we want absolute calculable knowledge]

will be able to control them and thereby become the "masters and possessors of nature" that Descartes envisioned. In Baconian terms, in gaining *knowledge* of nature, we gain *power* over nature.

Heidegger emphasizes how this knowledge of nature is related to the power interests of the subject in the sense that it makes nature something secure and stable:

> Insofar as it comes down to man as the subject, adequateness *secures* beings, and makes man certain of beings. Truth has become certainty and, through certainty, the securing of the constancy of the subject. This securing has to turn itself into a stabilization and the consolidation of beings, whereby it is no longer that important *what* each being is, *how* it shows itself. What is important, rather, is that beings surround us and are secured as something stable.[26]

This security and stability leads to the incredible advancements in technology that occur in the modern period. Heidegger states, "As one-sided and in many respects unsatisfactory as the interpretation of 'nature' as *res extensa* may be . . . it is the first resolute step through which modern machine technology . . . become[s] metaphysically possible for the first time."[27] Without the emphasis on the mathematical and the stipulation of viewing nature as a coherence of bodies in motion, the vast technological advances that occur during the modern period would be simply impossible according to Heidegger, since such exactitude provides unprecedented security in regard to our knowledge of objects. However, Heidegger himself is not interested in the technological advancements per se. Rather, he speaks about the essential unfolding [*Wesen*] of modern technology. In other words, Heidegger is interested about the way in which entities appear with the onset of modern technology rather than the technological advancements themselves. He states, for instance, "Our age is not a technological age because it is the age of the machine; it is an age of the machine because it is the technological age."[28] The current age, which we can call the contemporary period, is an era in which entities begin to show up differently. As we gain more and more knowledge of "nature" and gain an increasing mastery of nature, we enter into the contemporary period wherein "everything must be adjusted to the existing state of calculation . . . The incalculable is here only what has not yet been mastered by calculation."[29] In other words, we enter into an age wherein the calculating itself and the mastery that goes with it become more essential than what is calculated or mastered. Heidegger calls this period the age of modern technology. Since it is based on the metaphysical underpinnings set during the early modern period initiated by Descartes and is dependent upon the emphasis on the mathematical that eventually guides modern science, Heidegger considers the age of modern technology to be in line with the modern epoch, though there are notable differences between the early phases of the modern

mastery becomes more important than the thing mastered

epoch and the contemporary period as the age of modern technology. In the contemporary age of modern technology, our knowledge becomes so powerful that we attain a mastery over nature to such an extent that entities come to be seen as mere materials on hand for human consumption, i.e., as standing-reserve. In other words, as the mastery of the earth increases, the objects eventually no longer *ob-ject* to human interests, and all of nature is turned into a giant grid of energy to be on hand for human consumption and manipulated according to human interests. In the age of modern technology, human interests of mastery and security take precedence over respecting natural things as they are in themselves.

THE AGE OF MODERN TECHNOLOGY

Heidegger's most famous essay on the age of modern technology is his 1949 essay, "The Question Concerning Technology." Here, he offers his mature thoughts on the essential unfolding of the modern technological age of enframing [*Ge-stell*] wherein all entities are understood as standing-reserve. The first extensive reflection on the influence of modern science and technology and how they are intertwined, however, comes in his unpublished notes written from 1936 to 1939, which have been published under the titles *Contributions to Philosophy (From Enowning)* [*Beiträge zur Philosophie (Vom Ereignis)*] and *Mindfulness* [*Besinnung*]. In these works, Heidegger laments the one-sidedness of the modern scientific understanding that has assumed sovereign power in the Western world. He states, "modern science claims to be one or even *the* decisive knowing"[30] and, as modern science gains ultimate control and power, we enter into what he calls the age of "machination" [*Machenschaft*][31] wherein nothing "is any longer impossible and inaccessible. Everything 'is done' and 'can be done' if one only has the will for it."[32] With the success of science and the concomitant rise of technology, humans begin to believe that they have control over everything and can accomplish anything that they wish. Here, we can see the correlation between knowledge and power that Bacon noted in the modern period. As we gain more and more knowledge of nature through precisely measuring its coordinates and tendencies, we gain a greater potential of mastering over it and eventually manipulating it to our own interests of power. Eventually, we attain such heights that we no longer recognize limits to our power and view everything as capable of being mastered. This begins the age of machination, which can be succinctly captured by the common proverb, "Where there's a will, there's a way."

Heidegger defines machination as "that interpretation of beings as re-presentable and re-presented."[33] When humans begin to see all of reality in terms of machination, "only the representable *is*."[34] Here, we can see the influence of Cartesian metaphysics. In setting the standard of truth as anything that can be clearly and distinctly perceived by a subject, Cartesian metaphysics equates truth with whatever can be *represented* clearly and distinctly. Heidegger states, "The step taken by Descartes is already a first and decisive consequence, a 'compliance' by which machination assumes power as transformed truth (correctness), namely as certainty."[35] As clear and distinct, i.e., as *certain*, representation becomes the *only* standard of truth, Heidegger says that we become closed off to other possible ways in which entities come to presence. The problem that arises from this is that "everything presses forth into calculation, usage, . . . manageability, and regulation"[36] and, as we get more and more successful at representing the natural world with exactitude (thereby increasing our *knowledge*) and manipulating it to our interests (thereby increasing our *power*), "everything is open to and nothing is impossible for machination."[37] Humans believe themselves to be in ultimate control of nature, and find no limit to their control. In speaking to this, Heidegger states, "There is in principle no 'impossible'; one 'hates' this word; everything is humanly possible, if only everything is taken into account in advance, in every aspect, and if the conditions are furnished."[38] In other words, as long as our mathematical representation of nature is rigorous, precise, and all-inclusive, we can manipulate nature according to our interests. We can think of machination as the all-inclusive rubric of understanding things in terms of the subject's interests. In explaining it, Heidegger states, "Everything is now trapped in planned steerability and exactitude of a secure execution and an *'exhaustive' control*."[39]

When machination takes over as the decisive knowing, Heidegger says that we enter into the age of modern technology, and he gives us a clue as to how the age of modern technology comes to fruition in the following passage:

> As the form of the fundamental effectiveness of their machination, the created beings (highways, aircraft hangars at airports, giant ski-jumps, power stations and reservoirs, manufacturing plants and fortifications) are, in a different way than up to now, *fully eased into what is not their component, that is, into "what is," into "nature" and into the public "world."* "Nature" transforms itself according to these "installations," plants itself entirely into them and *comes to light only in them* and is held in their purview.[40]

When highways and power stations come to be seen as just as ordinary, commonplace, or "natural" as forests and prairies, Heidegger believes we are on our way to viewing all that *is* through the lens of machination. Moreover, the highway and the power station are creations of humans *for humans*, and nature soon comes to be seen in the same light. Of course, humans realize that they did not literally create nature; but nature seen as a conglomerate of objects that

We "re-present" natural objects as materials for our own use

can be calculated and manipulated is nature as represented or "created" by the human subject. And, as this becomes our "natural" understanding of things, nature itself becomes a creation of humans for humans, just like the highway and the power station. Here, we can see the relation to the earlier Greek idea of being as οὐσία. We mentioned in the last chapter that the dominant way in which the Greeks came to understand being was that of enduring presence, and this enduring presence was understood as οὐσία. As Heidegger notes, beings in the sense of οὐσία come to be seen as entities at one's disposal. He states, "These beings stand at one's disposal because they are fixed and stable, because they are *constantly attainable and at hand*."[41] When all beings are understood as entities created by the subject (whether literally or conceptually), the idea that humans are in complete control of them comes to dominate.

In the age of modern technology, Heidegger states that an anthropomorphism takes hold *wherein all that is* is *only as created by humans*: "Anthropomorphism is an explicit or implicit, acknowledged or unknowingly adopted conviction that 'beings in the whole' are what they are and how they are by virtue of, and in accordance with, the representation [of humans]."[42] Since our understanding of reality comes to be a representation of the world that is guided by the aims of certainty, security, and mastery, our experience of nature is *morphed* or changed to conform to our representation of it. As anthropomorphism takes hold, "what is named and known as a being is a human contrivance."[43] Moreover, the distinction between what is "human-made" and "natural" no longer holds any genuine weight when anthropomorphism reigns, since all is a creation or production of humans. We believe that we can, in principle, understand everything there is about anything at all if we simply put our minds to it, since all objects are understood in the Cartesian sense of quantifiable bodies of mass in space and time.

Heidegger tries to capture the extraordinary power that humans come to have over nature in his idea of the gigantic [*das Riesenhafte*].[44] He states, "The gigantic unfolds in the calculative and thus always manifests in the 'quantitative,' the *unconditioned domination* of representing and producing."[45] Daniela Vallega-Neu provides the following gloss on this term: "In the gigantic beings are discovered through their boundless calculability and makeability. Any being is always already discovered as quantitatively calculable."[46] Since the being of an entity *is* simply its extension in space and time, humans come to see themselves as gaining exhaustive knowledge of any entity when its spatiotemporal coordinates are calculated. Moreover, if all spatiotemporal coordinates have been exhaustively grasped, humans can be said to have attained exhaustive knowledge of the natural world. Understanding all entities in terms of their spatiotemporal coordinates takes away any distinctiveness or uniqueness about entities, since what the entities really are is understood on this basis alone. Heidegger puts this point in the following

[handwritten: things no longer seen as unique]

way: "[The gigantic] is no longer the re-presentable objectness of an unlimited quantification but rather quantity as quality."[47] What this means is that any qualitative differences between objects disappears when the emphasis is strictly on quantitative measurement.

In seeing everything as quantitatively calculable, Heidegger says that humans have completely gotten away from understanding nature as φύσις.[48] Nature is now "ultimately reduced to the full force of calculating machination and economy. And finally what [is] left [is] only 'scenery' and recreational opportunity and even this still calculated into the gigantic."[49] In other words, in the gigantic, absolutely everything "natural" has lost any sense of naturalness. In his analysis on Heidegger's understanding of the period of modern technology, Foltz states, "Technology attempts to master nature not merely by assuming control over natural things but above all by attempting to surmount its very tendencies of self-emerging—by contriving to overcome the kind of revealing (φύσις) that renders 'natural' the things of nature themselves."[50] The idea that entities self-emerge in their own unique ways no longer holds when anything and everything is seen as quantitatively calculable in an exhaustive manner. Eventually, the whole notion of experiencing nature on its own terms no longer can be taken seriously. We can think about this in terms of the most pristine types of wilderness areas that still exist in the world: national parks. Heidegger would say that even national parks where humans can seemingly enjoy the wilderness as it is in itself do not escape the all-inclusive calculating machination, since they are viewed as areas that must be managed by human beings. As they come to be understood as mere places of scenery or recreational opportunities, they are subsumed into the rubric of machination, since they come to be seen solely in terms of human interests.[51]

[handwritten left margin: to create a new kind of emerging that we can control]

We pointed out how the Greek understanding of being as οὐσία is related to the idea of machination. Vallega-Neu points out, however, that "machination becomes more dominant in the Middle Ages through the Judeo-Christian notion of creation; all beings are *made* by God and thus become explainable according to the schema of cause and effect."[52] This schema of cause and effect is carried over into the modern period. Essentially, during the modern period, a shift occurs regarding who makes or creates beings. Instead of viewing entities as created by God, they are now created (at least conceptually, if not literally) by the human subject. Moreover, as forms of technological devices become increasingly intertwined with our everyday lives and our day-to-day routines include them, we come to have a greater sense of mastery of the world around us, since these devices allow us to dictate to nature how we function within it, rather than the other way around. Lee Braver puts this point in the following way: "Thanks to modern technology, I no longer need to regulate my desires and activities to conform to the seasons or whims of nature."[53] For instance, instead of having to wait for the proper time of year in which the harvest is ready in order to eat certain foods, we can simply inject them with preservatives and enjoy them year-round.

Heidegger's ideas of the gigantic and machination reach their maturation in his 1949 essay, "The Question Concerning Technology," when he begins to think of the essential unfolding of the modern technological age as *Gestell*, which is commonly translated as "enframing." Heidegger himself equates machination with enframing in the late 1930s, so we can see that Heidegger sees a link between the two concepts.[54] We can think of enframing as the combination of his earlier ideas of machination and the gigantic, since it is based on the idea that everything that exists does so as represented by humans (in the sense of machination), and that this way of revealing entities gains unconditional domination (through the gigantic). At the same time, however, Heidegger adds some aspects to his idea of enframing that cannot be found in his earlier work.

ENFRAMING AS THE ESSENTIAL UNFOLDING OF MODERN TECHNOLOGY

In the contemporary period known as the age of modern technology, everything that exists comes to be seen merely as a resource. As the modern scientific model takes over as *the* model of attaining truth, the objects that the subject once attempted to understand and manipulate are replaced with the standing-reserve (*Bestand*), which can be understood as a "stock" or "inventory" of material on hand to be maximally utilized and optimized. Objects no longer have the character of standing-against that they did early in the modern period, since their "otherness" or "standing-againstness" has been conquered. There is no longer anything mysterious or unique about any entity in the contemporary period because everything can be completely calculated and therefore manipulated. As modern science and technology emerge and master everything that was once seen as other, the objects become completely calculable and interchangeable units of energy in the contemporary period and are thereby seen as merely undifferentiated material on hand to be exploited. Now, nature is revealed in a new way: "The revealing that rules in modern technology is a challenging [*Herausfordern*], which puts to nature the demand that it supply energy that can be extracted and stored as such."[55] With the onset of this new way of revealing that takes hold, everything that *is* is revealed in terms of standing-reserve, and nature becomes a grid of energy for exploitation.

We can see a distinct relation to Heidegger's earlier writings on machination in "The Question Concerning Technology." Just as Heidegger argues that people lose the sense of the distinction between what is human-made and natural with the onset of machination and anthropomorphism in *Contributions to Philosophy* and *Mindfulness*, Heidegger argues that everything is subsumed into the rubric of resourcefulness in this later essay. He argues, for instance, that there is fundamentally no distinction between a power station and a river anymore, since they are both viewed as resources of energy and nothing more. Heidegger states that "even the Rhine itself appears as something at our command. . . . The river is dammed up into the power plant. What the river is now, namely, a water power supplier, derives from out of the essence of the power station."[56] The river is no longer seen in its own natural terms as in ancient Greece, as a creation of God as in the Middle Ages, or even as an object standing against the knowing subject as in the modern period; the river is now seen as just another part of the giant, undifferentiated grid of energy. Just as the river is viewed strictly in terms of its energy efficiency and resourcefulness, so are all other entities. As Heidegger states, "the earth now reveals itself as a coal mining district, the soil as a mineral deposit, . . . agriculture is now the mechanized food industry,"[57] and "nature becomes a gigantic gasoline station, an energy source for modern technology and industry."[58] Instead of viewing nature as a conglomerate of objects in space and time, nature comes to be viewed as an undifferentiated grid of energy to be unlocked, stored up, and exploited due to the tremendous success of modern science and modern technology, which are both based primarily on Cartesian metaphysics and the emphasis on the mathematical.

Although the contemporary age of modern technology finds its metaphysical underpinnings in the modern period, there is a major difference between the two. The fundamental difference between the modern period as initiated by Descartes and the contemporary period of enframing is that the subject and objects are both "sucked up" into the realm of standing-reserve during the contemporary period. Heidegger states, "When man, investigating, observing, ensnares nature as an area of his own conceiving, he has already been claimed by a way of revealing that challenges him to approach nature as an object of research, until *even the object disappears into the objectlessness of standing-reserve.*"[59] While entities had the quality of standing-against in the modern period since they were still somewhat mysterious (i.e., we still had a ways to go in becoming the "masters and possessors of nature" that Descartes envisioned), they no longer have the quality of standing-against in the contemporary period because they are understood merely as an undifferentiated grid of energy that completely acquiesces to human interests. The rivers, soils, winds, and the sun are seen as power suppliers and have no distinctive standing of their own but are rather mere constituents of the giant energy grid. Also, since a subject only makes sense in distinction to an object (recall the German word for "object," *Gegenstand*), the "special Subject" that we saw in the modern period also disappears. Heidegger argues, "As soon as what is unconcealed no longer concerns man even as object, but does so, rather, exclusively as standing-reserve, and man in the midst of objectless is nothing but the orderer of the standing-reserve, then he comes to the very brink of a precipitous fall; that is, *he comes to the point where he himself will have to be taken as standing-reserve.*"[60] The Cartesian subject who once determined the measure of reality by focusing on what can be clearly and distinctly perceived (i.e., extended objects in space and time) no longer stands as opposed to the objects but rather is seen as standing-reserve as well. Instead of being the special subjects who underlie all of reality by determining the measure of what counts as in being, the only legitimate measure comes to be seen in terms of resourcefulness, and the possibility arises that humans are seen as resources as well. Heidegger states, "The current talk of human *resources*, about the *supply* of patients for a clinic, gives evidence of this."[61] The fact that we see the term "human resources" as a part of our everyday, common parlance is a sign that enframing has taken hold. Like the Rhine, humans come to be viewed in terms of productivity. At the same time, however, since humans still take part in the ordering of the standing-reserve (e.g., we choose which resources are the most resourceful), humans should never be seen as merely standing-reserve. We will see in chapter 4 how understanding human beings as merely elements of the standing-reserve or as mere orderers of the standing-reserve is simply inappropriate. For now, let us gain a better understanding of what enframing means.

Heidegger defines enframing as "the gathering together of that setting-upon which sets upon man, i.e., challenges him forth, to reveal the real, in the mode of ordering, as standing-reserve."[62] The word "enframing" is the translation of the German word "*Ge-stell*," which, as Iain Thomson notes, "etymologically [connotes] a *gathering together* ('*Ge-*') of the myriad forms of *stellen* ('to set, stand, regulate, secure, ready, establish,' and so on)."[63] Enframing is the way in which everything is framed together in an undifferentiated mass of energy: the standing-reserve. While humans used to represent (*vor-stellen*) objects in accordance with their interests of certainty and security, everything is now gathered-together-to-stand (*Ge-stell*) as standing-reserve, and this is the only sort of revealing that reigns in the contemporary period. Moreover, humans come to be challenged to view reality strictly in these terms. Heidegger states that the challenging of enframing "sets upon man to order the real as standing-reserve."[64] Because enframing becomes the all-inclusive rubric of understanding entities, humans are challenged to order reality in this particular fashion, which cuts off any other ways in which to arrange the world.

Since enframing becomes the only mode of unconcealment in the contemporary period that is marked by modern industrial and *technological* progress, Heidegger says that "the essence of modern technology lies in enframing."[65]

He continues, "everywhere everything is ordered to stand by, to be immediately at hand, indeed to stand there just so that it may be on call for a further ordering."[66] We should point out that the word "essence" in the phrase "the essence of modern technology" is the translation of the German term "*Wesen*," which has a specific meaning for Heidegger. He understands *Wesen* as the way in which something essentially unfolds, which does not have to do with industrial, scientific, or technological progress itself. Rather, the essential unfolding of the contemporary age of modern technology lies in the way in which entities come to be viewed and understood as standing-reserve. *To be* an entity in this period is to be a part of the standing-reserve, and to be a part of the standing-reserve is to be understood as an aspect of the "inclusive rubric"[67] of energy that is stored up and therefore is on hand to be exploited.

Considering this, as we did in speaking about the difference between science and scientism, we must be sure to make a distinction between modern technology and the essential unfolding of modern technology when speaking of the age of modern technology. As Braver states, "What Heidegger means by technology is straightforward: machines that perform tasks with greater efficiency than human hands."[68] Heidegger makes it clear that he does not have any problem with technology as such. He states, "For all of us, the arrangements, devices, and machinery of technology are to a greater or lesser extent indispensable. It would be foolish to attack technology blindly. It would be shortsighted to condemn it as the work of the devil."[69] Just as Heidegger does not have a problem with science as such, he is not a Luddite who yearns for a society devoid of modern technology. At the same time, however, Heidegger does see the rise of modern technology to be accompanied by the age of enframing in which there is only one sort of revealing of entities, and this is where he sees the problem. Heidegger makes this clear early on in "The Question Concerning Technology" in his discussion of τέχνη [*techne*], the Greek word from which our word "technology" is derived. Here, he points out that τέχνη is associated with "the activities and skills of the craftsman"[70] and is commonly understood as the "know-how" that is associated with these activities.[71] While Heidegger admits that this is the usual understanding of the term, he states that this is not the essence [*Wesen*] of τέχνη. He states, "What is decisive in *techne* does not lie at all in making and manipulating nor in the using of means, but rather in the . . . revealing. It is as revealing, and not as manufacturing, that τέχνη is a bringing-forth."[72] Heidegger states that the craftsman who creates a house or a ship brings forth a new way in which the materials are revealed and understood. Instead of a collection of raw materials, for example, one experiences a ship to sail or a house in which to reside. In this sense, τέχνη is a mode of revealing, since it brings about a new way of understanding entities.

technology reveals entities in new way
& orients materials

Heidegger argues that the essential unfolding of modern technology is similar in that it is a revealing. This is why he tries to distinguish between the essential unfolding of modern technology and technological devices as such. For Heidegger, the essential unfolding of modern technology lies in enframing, though "enframing . . . is nothing technological, nothing on the order of a machine. It is the way in which the real reveals itself as standing-reserve."[73] Heidegger spells this out in speaking of the difference between specific technological advances that were particularly troubling during his lifetime, such as the atomic bomb.[74] The problem is not that the modern technological revolution brings about technological advances that threaten the existence of human civilizations (such as the atomic bomb); rather, for Heidegger, the problem is that we begin to view everything strictly as standing-reserve and are not open to other ways in which entities can be understood. Heidegger states, "The rule of enframing threatens man with the possibility that it could be denied to him to enter into a *more original revealing*."[75] Heidegger believes that enframing may take such a hold that we will forget that there are other more appropriate ways in which entities can reveal themselves (such as what we saw in the pre-Socratic understandings of being). Much of his later thought deals with what a more appropriate sort of revealing might look like.

ENFRAMING AND THE CLIMATE CRISIS

Before we can engage with Heidegger's understanding of a more appropriate revealing of entities, we must show the link between the climate crisis and enframing. The climate crisis is visibly linked with the mastery over the earth that accompanies enframing. The Industrial Revolution is the clear beginning marker of anthropogenic climate change, since it initiates the fossil fuel–based economy that has come to dominate the contemporary period. While coal was the primary energy source during the early parts of the modern period, oil quickly became the most important resource in the world when people began to see the high energy density of oil compared to coal. This led to what Leonardo Maugeri calls "the age of gasoline and oil imperialism" in the twentieth century in which Western companies strove to acquire as much of the extractable oil resources on the planet as they possibly could.[76] In the early 2000s, environmentalists warned that we had hit global peak oil, which can be defined as "that moment in time when the world will achieve its maximum possible rate of oil extraction; from then on for reasons having mostly to do with geology, the amount of petroleum available to society on a daily or yearly basis will begin to dwindle."[77] However, humans found a way to continue with the fossil fuel–based society by finding innovative ways to get at hard-to-access oil with new technologies such as horizontal and offshore drilling, which are both clearly instantiations of the "where there is a will, there is a way" sort of thinking that typifies the age of modern technology. Even clearer illustrations of enframing can be seen with the techniques of hydraulic fracturing or "fracking" in which pressurized water is used to fracture dense shale formations to get at oil and natural gas or the notoriously energy-intensive techniques used to reach the oil in bituminous tar sands.[78] Despite the clear scientific link between fossil fuel consumption and climate change, and the detrimental effects on human health and habitats noted in chapter 1, these technologies prove that mastery and production have come to trump even human well-being and thus are what ultimately matter the most.

Indeed, many of the proposals to respond to the climate crisis are caught up in the same sort of thinking that has caused the crisis in the first place. In 1854, the great environmental philosopher Henry David Thoreau argued that "man is an animal who more than any other can adapt himself to all climates and circumstances."[79] Thoreau is surely correct, though the climate crisis threatens the ability for the human species to adapt to climate change and the harsher world that it entails. Therefore, scientists and engineers are considering several responses, and the most pervasive technological response to climate change is geoengineering. In geoengineering, the goal is explicitly to reengineer the planet in accordance with human interests. Some examples of direct approaches to climate change include carbon dioxide removal (CDR) and the use of solar radiation management (SRM). Regarding CDR, carbon capture and storage (CCS) is a proposed technological solution in which the carbon dioxide that would otherwise drift off into the atmosphere is captured and routed deep into the earth's geological repositories such as depleted oil and gas reservoirs. Technological concerns still surround this proposal, as a breach in the repositories would result in a significant release of carbon dioxide all at once and a large-scale, rapid approach could negatively affect plants' ability to adapt, since carbon dioxide is essential to their respiration.[80] Nevertheless, CCS is being pursued experimentally and will be technologically viable by 2020.[81] SRM is a geoengineering technique on a larger scale than CDR since it entails a literal reconfiguration of the atmosphere. There are several proposals in line with SRM, but the most popular one is the injection of sulfate aerosols into the stratosphere to mimic a volcanic eruption, thereby cooling the climate. Crutzen explains this technology in the following manner: "Anthropogenically enhanced sulfate particle concentrations . . . cool the planet, offsetting [a] fraction of the anthropogenic increase in greenhouse gas warming."[82] Like CDR, there are risks associated with SRM, since changing the chemistry balance of the atmosphere will likely affect weather patterns by increasing the number of droughts and decreasing amounts of precipitation.[83] However, sulfate aerosol injection has been called "the most feasible geoengineering option" due to the known effects of volcanic eruptions on the earth's climate.[84]

From a Heideggerian perspective, the question is not how efficient and safe CDR and SRM technologies can be, but rather what enacting such technologies says about the human being and the way in which humans approach nature. CDR essentially allows human beings to continue with business as usual and simply put our faith in technology, while SRM crowns human beings as masters of the natural world in that even the amount of energy the earth receives from the sun can be managed. This only proves Heidegger's thesis that "there is no impossible" for the modern human being in the age of enframing. *Everything* can be managed as long as there is the will to do so.

In chapter 1, we noted the clear link between climate change and resource depletions such as water, forests, and food. As with the geoengineering solutions to climate change, humans have found technological ways to respond to resource depletions. In regard to water, desalination technologies have been enacted that convert saltwater into potable water. Although such technologies are energy intensive, severe droughts caused by climate change have forced some regions to enact such measures.[85] In regard to forests, deforestation has prompted massive research into genetically enhanced trees. For instance, a scientist at Columbia University "proposes to build millions of 'artificial trees' that would be a thousand times more efficient than real ones at taking carbon from the atmosphere," thereby "improving nature."[86] Finally, in regard to food depletions, genetically modified foods, which were introduced in 1996, have been called "the fastest adopted crop technology in the history of modern agriculture."[87] All of these approaches re*make* the world into the image of the human being in that when the natural world is insufficient in supplying resources, human beings use their ingenuity and ambition to create resources artificially. When the world has become a repository of mere resources, it doesn't much matter whether these resources are natural or *man*ufactured. Perhaps the best quote that encapsulates the way in which human beings approach the climate crisis and the concomitant resource depletions comes from Larry Summers, former chief economist for the World Bank and economic advisor to the White House under both President Clinton and President Obama, who states, "There are no limits to the carrying capacity of the earth that are likely to bind any time in the foreseeable future. There isn't a risk of an apocalypse due to global warming or anything else. *The idea that we should put limits on growth because of some natural limit is a profound error*."[88] Underlying this quote is not only the idea that the world simply is a vast array of resources for humans to utilize, therefore in line with enframing, but also the idea that humans should not recognize any limits to their capability of utilizing these resources, thereby in line with Heidegger's idea that modern humanity "recognizes no limit in the given, and *wants* to find no limit,"[89] which Heidegger states in his discussion of the gigantic. Here, Summers blatantly expresses his trust in the human ability to conquer nature, regardless of the circumstances. Moreover, he shows that the emphasis should always be placed on human interests.

From an eco-phenomenological perspective, a massive change in our understanding of what it means *to be* must take place in order for us to usher in a sustainable future for the natural world and the human place within it. Heidegger himself agreed with this, though he had little faith in the ability for humans to enact a change in the course of the history of being, since he often saw enframing as a natural outcome of the beginnings set in ancient Greece. For instance, he stated that machination "does not name a human comportment but a manner of the essential swaying of being."[90] Moreover, Heidegger considered the modern technological age to coincide with the term "completed metaphysics."[91] Basically, Heidegger believed that machination and enframing were a part of the essential unfolding of Western metaphysics established in ancient Greece. Just as an oak tree naturally sprouts from an acorn, enframing was bound to come out of the early Greek understanding of being. This is why we find him saying that "only a god can save us"[92] or, even more bleakly, "Before being can occur in its primal truth, Being as the will must be broken, the world must be forced to collapse and the earth must be driven to desolation. . . . The laboring animal is left to the giddy whirl of its products so that it may tear itself to pieces and annihilate itself in empty nothingness."[93] What Heidegger is saying here is that the world must face an utter collapse in order to enact a new sort of revealing of entities. Until then, we will simply continue with the age of modern technology.

In certain points in Heidegger's corpus, however, his tone is a bit more hopeful. For instance, in *Contributions to Philosophy*, he asks, "Must nature be surrendered and abandoned to machination? Are we still capable of seeking earth anew?"[94] What Heidegger is asking is whether we can be open to different ways in which natural entities come to presence that are not immediately subsumed into the rubric of machination (or enframing). He spends much of his later thought trying to understand what a postmetaphysical understanding of entities might look like. Our task in the next chapter will be to utilize some of the elements of this postmetaphysical understanding of being that Heidegger points to in order to comprise an environmentally sustainable understanding of the human place in the world.

NOTES

1. On Aristotle's influence, see especially *The Cambridge History of Later Medieval Philosophy: From the Rediscovery of Aristotle to the Disintegration of Scholasticism: 1100–1600*, ed. Norman Kretzmann, Anthony Kenny, and Jan Pinborg (Cambridge: Cambridge University Press, 1982). We should point out from the start that science was not understood as a self-contained discipline in the medieval or early

modern period as it is now. Therefore, for our purposes, we can understand science during this period to include any type of activity that sought to understand the natural world.

2. As William Dampier notes, philosophers like Duns Scotus, William of Ockam, and Nicholas of Cusa all attempted to shake the influence of Aristotelian Scholasticism during the medieval period, but Aristotle's influence was still immense at the time of Bacon and Descartes. See Dampier's *A Shorter History of Science* (New York: Meridian Books, 1957), 58.

3. Herbert Butterfield, *The Origins of Modern Science: 1300–1800* (London: G. Bell and Sons, 1958), 97.

4. Butterfield, *The Origins of Modern Science*, 101.

5. Francis Bacon, *New Organon*, ed. Lisa Jardine and Michael Silverthorne (Cambridge: Cambridge University Press, 2000), 34, aphorism 8.

6. Bacon, *New Organon*, 36, aphorism 18.

7. René Descartes, "To Mersenne, On J.-B. Morin's Proof for the Existence of God (January 28, 1641)," in *René Descartes: Philosophical Essays and Correspondence*, ed. Roger Ariew (Indianapolis and Cambridge: Hackett Publishing Company, 2000), 96.

8. Lawrence M. Principe, *Scientific Revolution: A Very Short Introduction* (Oxford: Oxford University Press, 2011), 79.

9. Heidegger, *What Is a Thing?* 97 [GA 41, 98].

10. Heidegger, *What Is a Thing?* 70 [GA 41, 71].

11. Heidegger, *What Is a Thing?* 73 [GA 41, 73]. Liddell and Scott define μάθημα [*mathema*] as "that which is learnt, a lesson" in the *Greek-English Lexicon*, 483. The word μαθητός [*mathetos*] is translated as "that may be learnt," which seems to offer a better validation for Heidegger's claim.

12. Heidegger, *What Is a Thing?* 75 [GA 41, 76].

13. Descartes, *Rules for the Direction of the Mind*, 3 (my emphasis).

14. Heidegger, *What Is a Thing?* 101 [GA 41, 101].

15. Heidegger, *What Is a Thing?* 103 [GA 41, 104].

16. Cf. Heidegger, *What Is a Thing?* 101 [GA 41, 101].

17. Heidegger examines Descartes' understanding of the being of beings in *Being and Time*, 122–125 [GA 2, 119–123] with his analysis of Descartes' view of *extensio*. Here, he points out that the Latin term *extensio* means "that which can be measured."

18. Heidegger, *What Is a Thing?* 81 [GA 41, 81]. Heidegger is quoting from Aristotle's *De Caelo* [On the Heavens], 306a.

19. Heidegger, *What Is a Thing?* 83 [GA 41, 84].

20. Heidegger, *What Is a Thing?* 80 [GA 41, 81].

21. For the understanding of inner principles in the medieval period, see Steven P. Marrone's "Medieval Philosophy in Context," in *The Cambridge Companion to Medieval Philosophy*, ed. Arthur Stephen McGrade (Cambridge: Cambridge University Press, 2003), 32–36.

22. This is especially true with the onset of Newtonian mechanics.

23. Although I am admittedly grouping the Cartesian and Baconian methodologies together, David Oldroyd points out that the methods of Bacon and Descartes were actually quite different. He states that while Bacon preferred "the upward inductive

movement from a wide empirical base," Descartes "tended to emphasize the downward, deductive, 'rational' aspects of scientific enquiry" (*The Arch of Knowledge*, 67). The details of the methods of themselves are not important for our purposes. What is important is that both sought to overthrow Aristotelian science and emphasized the mathematical in doing so.

24. Heidegger, *What Is a Thing?* 41 [GA 41, 40] (my emphasis).

25. Heidegger, "The Age of the World Picture," 119 [GA 5, 79] (my emphasis).

26. Martin Heidegger, *Mindfulness*, 92 [GA 66, 110].

27. Heidegger, *Nietzsche, Volume IV*, 116 [GA 6.2, 164].

28. Heidegger, *What Is Called Thinking?* 24 [GA 8, 27].

29. Heidegger, *Contributions to Philosophy*, 84 [GA 65, 121].

30. Heidegger, *Contributions to Philosophy*, 98 [GA 65, 141]. Heidegger says something similar to this in his essay, "On the Question of Being." Here he states, "The representational activity of the sciences everywhere concerns beings, and indeed special regions of beings . . . [The sciences] are of the opinion that the representation of beings exhausts the entire realm of what can be researched and questioned, and that apart from beings there is 'nothing else.'" Cf. Heidegger, *Pathmarks*, 316 [GA 9, 418].

31. Heidegger's term *Machenschaft* is a neologism. The plural form of this German word is, however, a common term. *Machenschaften* means "machinations" or "wheelings and dealings" (in the negative sense of corrupt business practices, for instance). Heidegger explicitly distances his way of using this term from the common one in *Contributions to Philosophy*, 88 [GA 65, 126].

32. Heidegger, *Contributions to Philosophy*, 76 [GA 65, 108] (translation modified). The original German translated as "Everything 'is done' and 'can be done'" is "*Alles, wird gemacht' und 'läßt sich machen.'*"

33. Heidegger, *Contributions to Philosophy*, 76 [GA 65, 109].

34. Heidegger, *Contributions to Philosophy*, 76 [GA 65, 109].

35. Heidegger, *Contributions to Philosophy*, 92 [GA 65, 132]. Notice here that Heidegger uses the word "consequence." Heidegger does not believe that Descartes initiates the age of machination; rather, machination "has been effectively in operation since the first beginning of Western thinking [in ancient Greece]" (*Contributions to Philosophy*, 92 [GA 65, 132]).

36. Heidegger, *Contributions to Philosophy*, 87 [GA 65, 124].

37. Heidegger, *Contributions to Philosophy*, 91 [GA 65, 131].

38. Heidegger, *Contributions to Philosophy*, 95 [GA 65, 136].

39. Heidegger, *Contributions to Philosophy*, 286 [GA 65, 406] (my emphasis).

40. Heidegger, *Mindfulness*, 23 [GA 66, 30] (my emphasis).

41. Martin Heidegger, *The Essence of Human Freedom: An Introduction to Philosophy*, trans. Ted Sadler (New York and London: Continuum, 2002), 36 [GA 31, 51].

42. Heidegger, *Mindfulness*, 137 [GA 66, 159]. We normally use the term "anthropomorphic" when speaking of attributing human characteristics to nonhuman entities, as can be seen in the phrases "the sea was angry" and "the sky was calm." Heidegger's use of this term is in line with this usage, but deals with nature as a whole, rather than its individual constituents.

43. Heidegger, *Mindfulness*, 137 [GA 66, 159].

44. Stuart Elden points out that Heidegger's critique of *das Riesenhafte* may have political dimensions, pointing out that "the Behemoth that became the symbol of the Nazi war machine" is a candidate for what Heidegger has in mind in his discussion of this concept. See his "Contributions to Geography? The Spaces of Heidegger's *Beiträge*," *Environment and Planning D: Society and Space* (2005, volume 23, 811–827): 817. Looking specifically at the text, however, I think that my broader interpretation of this concept is appropriate.

45. Heidegger, *Contributions to Philosophy*, 311 [GA 65, 442] (my emphasis).

46. Daniela Vallega-Neu, *Heidegger's* Contributions to Philosophy: *An Introduction* (Bloomington and Indianapolis: Indiana University Press, 2003), 61.

47. Heidegger, *Contributions to Philosophy*, 94 [GA 65, 135].

48. Cf. Heidegger, *Contributions to Philosophy*, 94 [GA 65, 135].

49. Heidegger, *Contributions to Philosophy*, 195 [GA 65, 277].

50. Foltz, *Inhabiting the Earth*, 102.

51. Heidegger doesn't speak about national parks explicitly, but he says something similar in "The Question Concerning Technology" about the Rhine River. He states, for instance, that the Rhine becomes "an object on call for inspection by a tour group ordered there by the vacation industry" (16 [GA 7, 17]).

52. Vallega-Neu, *Heidegger's* Contributions to Philosophy, 60.

53. Lee Braver, *Heidegger's Later Writings: A Reader's Guide* (London and New York: Continuum, 2009), 85.

54. Cf. "Sketches for a History of Being as Metaphysics" in *The End of Philosophy*, trans. Joan Stambaugh (Chicago: The University of Chicago Press, 1973), 66 [GA 6.2, 471].

55. Heidegger, "The Question Concerning Technology," 14 [GA 7, 15] (translation modified).

56. Heidegger, "The Question Concerning Technology," 16 [GA 7, 16].

57. Heidegger, "The Question Concerning Technology," 14–16 [GA 7, 15–17].

58. Heidegger, *Discourse on Thinking*, 50 [GA 16, 523].

59. Heidegger, "The Question Concerning Technology," 19 [GA 7, 19].

60. Heidegger, "The Question Concerning Technology," 26–27 [GA 7, 27–28] (my emphasis).

61. Heidegger, "The Question Concerning Technology," 18 [GA 7, 18] (my emphasis).

62. Heidegger, "The Question Concerning Technology," 20 [GA 7, 21].

63. Thomson, *Heidegger on Ontotheology*, 53.

64. Heidegger, "The Question Concerning Technology," 19 [GA 7, 20].

65. Heidegger, "The Question Concerning Technology," 23 [GA 7, 24].

66. Heidegger, "The Question Concerning Technology," 17 [GA 7, 17].

67. Heidegger, "The Question Concerning Technology," 17 [GA 7, 17].

68. Braver, *Heidegger's Later Writings*, 82.

69. Heidegger, *Discourse on Thinking*, 53 [GA 16, 526].

70. Heidegger, "The Question Concerning Technology," 13 [GA 7, 14].

71. Liddell and Scott translate τέχνη as "art, skill, craft in work" (*Greek-English Lexicon*, 804).

72. Heidegger, "The Question Concerning Technology," 13 [GA 7, 14].

73. Heidegger, "The Question Concerning Technology," 23 [GA 7, 24].

74. Cf. Martin Heidegger, "What Are Poets For?" in *Poetry, Language, Thought*, trans. Albert Hofstadter (New York: Harper and Row, 1971), 116–117 [GA 5, 294].

75. Heidegger, "The Question Concerning Technology," 28 [GA 7, 29].

76. Cf. Leonardo Maugeri, *The Age of Oil: The Mythology, History, and Future of the World's Most Controversial Resource* (Westport, Conn.: Praeger, 2006), chapter 2.

77. Richard Heinberg, *Peak Everything: Waking Up to the Century of Declines* (Gabriola Island, BC, Canada: New Society, 2007), 1.

78. Cf. *The Human and Environmental Impact of Fracking: How Fracturing Shale for Gas Affects Us and Our World*, ed. Madelon Lubin Finkel (Santa Barbara, Denver, and Oxford: Prager, 2015) and Andrew Nikiforuk, *Tar Sands: Dirty Oil and the Future of a Continent*, revised and updated (Vancouver: D&M Publishers, 2010).

79. Henry David Thoreau, *Walden* (Secaucus, N.J.: Longriver Press, 1976), 54.

80. For risks of CCS, see Naomi E. Vaughan and Timothy M. Lenton, "A Review of Climate Geoengineering Proposals," *Climatic Change* 109, no. 3 (2011): 758–761.

81. Cf. R. Stuart Haszeldine, "Carbon Capture and Storage: How Green Can Black Be?" *Science* 325, no. 5948 (2009): 1649.

82. Paul J. Crutzen, "Albedo Enhancement by Stratospheric Sulfur Injections: A Contribution to Resolve a Policy Dilemma?" *Climatic Change* 77, no. 3–4 (2006): 211.

83. Cf. Vaughan and Lenton, "A Review of Climate Geoengineering Proposals," 764–765.

84. Takanobu Kosugi, "Fail-Safe Solar Radiation Management Geoengineering." *Mitigation and Adaptation Strategies for Global Change* 18, no. 8 (2013): 1142.

85. Cf. Quirin Schiermeier, "Water: Purification with a Pinch of Salt," *Nature* 452, no. 7185 (2008): 260–261.

86. Fred Krupp and Miriam Horn, *Earth: The Sequel: The Race to Reinvent Energy and Stop Global Warming* (New York: W.W. Norton & Company, 2009), 250.

87. Gurdev S. Khush, "Genetically Modified Crops: The Fastest Adopted Crop Technology in the History of Modern Agriculture," *Agriculture & Food Security* 1, no. 14 (2012): 2.

88. Quoted from Bill McKibben, *Deep Economy: The Wealth of Communities and the Durable Future* (New York: St. Martin's Press, 2007), 24 (emphasis added).

89. Heidegger, *Contributions to Philosophy*, 95 [GA 65, 136].

90. Heidegger, *Contributions to Philosophy*, 88 [GA 65, 126].

91. Heidegger, "Overcoming Metaphysics," 93 [GA 7, 79].

92. Cf. "Only a God Can Save Us," 276.

93. Heidegger, "Overcoming Metaphysics," 86–87 [GA 7, 71].

94. Heidegger, *Contributions to Philosophy*, 195 [GA 65, 278].

Chapter Four

A New Way of Revealing

While Heidegger's most well-known work, *Being and Time*, is challenging but discernible through careful study, Heidegger's later philosophy is notoriously obscure and difficult to get any sort of firm grasp on. Despite this, I think that one thing is clear: the overarching aim of Heidegger's later thought is to critique the Western metaphysical tradition and attempt to offer a glimpse at what a new way of revealing entities might look like. In the last two chapters, we surveyed Western metaphysics and showed how enframing leads to the climate crisis. In this chapter, we will look at Heidegger's search for a new way of revealing entities. While scholars debate as to what exactly this new way of revelation entails, it is clear that Heidegger attempts to get away from anthropocentrism. Heidegger puts this point in the following way: "now the *great turning around* [*große Umkehrung*] is necessary . . . in which beings are not grounded in terms of human being, but rather human being is grounded in terms of be-ing [*Seyn*]."[1] In this great turning around, the aim is to get away from understanding all of reality strictly in terms of human interests. In order to do so, Heidegger shuns the idea that humans are created especially in God's image as we saw in the medieval epoch, the idea that reality should be determined by a human subject as we saw in the early modern epoch, or the idea that all of nature is a vast array of resources on hand for human consumption as we saw in the contemporary period. Heidegger often calls this *great turning around* a "new beginning" or the "other beginning" in that it will incite a change in the human relationship with being. Our task will be to attempt to understand what this new beginning could look like and how it can link up with a response to our environmental crisis.

THE NEW BEGINNING

Heidegger's vision of the great turnaround or new beginning results in "a complete transformation of relations to beings and to be-ing."[2] We noted in the previous chapter that Heidegger views enframing as a culmination of the Western metaphysical tradition. The ancient Greek understanding of beings as οὐσία, which, as we have seen, means "beings [that] stand at one's disposal because they are fixed and stable, because they are *constantly attainable and at hand*,"[3] eventually unfolds into the contemporary understanding of beings as standing-reserve. Here, everything is seen as energy-infused material on hand to be optimally utilized because it has become constantly attainable and able to be manipulated to our interests. We have seen how this has led to the environmental crisis in our analyses of climate change and resource deple- tions. Since our way of viewing the world infuses our ways of living upon it, in order to respond to this crisis, we must shift our understanding of reality, which requires either a new metaphysics or a postmetaphysical understanding of reality. Heidegger states that since metaphysics is "the presupposition of [the West's] planetary dominance,"[4] the only way to bring about this new beginning is to initiate a postmetaphysical understanding of reality, which he calls the new beginning. This new beginning is a radical departure from the previous epochs, though it somehow has a relation to the first beginning. While he notes that there is a "relation *to* the one and only first beginning [in ancient Greece]"[5] and that one must have a "reverence for the first begin- ning,"[6] he states, "in commencing a preparedness for crossing from the end of the first beginning into the other beginning, it is not as if man simply enters a 'period' that has not yet been, but it is rather that man enters a totally different domain of history."[7] Since all configurations of Western metaphysics are permutations from the initial understanding of reality as οὐσία, the goal is to move beyond these permutations altogether and initiate a new understanding of reality.[8] Heidegger states, "The path of thought of be-ing-historical thinking [*seynsgeschichtliche Denken*] runs outside any 'metaphysics,' whether ancient, Christian, or modern."[9] Heidegger is seeking nothing less than a radical shift in regard to how we view reality and the human place in nature.

In *Contributions to Philosophy*, Heidegger endeavors to move beyond metaphysics altogether. He states in the first few paragraphs that his aim is to cross from metaphysics into be-ing-historical thinking and "venture only an *attempt* to think according to a more originary basic stance within the ques- tion of the truth of be-ing."[10] Our task will be to offer a basic interpretation of what this be-ing-historical thinking might look like and then flesh out Heidegger's later notions of freedom [*Freiheit*], letting beings be [*Gelassen- heit*], and dwelling [*Wohnen*], all of which are elements of the new beginning that he envisions.

The main reason why Heidegger attempts to move beyond metaphysics is that humans in the contemporary period have forgotten the question of be-ing. Heidegger states, "Man with his machinations might for centuries yet pillage and lay waste to the planet, the gigantic character of this driving might 'develop' into something unimaginable and take on the form of a seeming rigor as the massive regulating of the desolate as such—yet the greatness of be-ing continues to be closed off."[11] Here, Heidegger is hinting that the way in which to get away from our pillaging of the planet is to step back and allow the "greatness of be-ing" to open up. In order to understand this quote, we need to get a grasp on Heidegger's later vision of be-ing. Heidegger's term *Seyn*, which is typically translated as "be-ing," is essential in understanding his postmetaphysical vision of how beings could be revealed in the new beginning. As Daniela Vallega-Neu notes, "For Heidegger, the use of the word '*Seyn*' [be-ing] (instead of '*Sein*' [being]) indicates that being is not thought of metaphysically."[12] Since enframing is a result of the Western metaphysical tradition as such, Heidegger's aim is to move beyond the Western metaphysical tradition, and be-ing is one of the keys in doing so. I will follow Polt's interpretation of this term; he states that "Heidegger's *Seyn* . . . is best interpreted as the giving of being, that is, as the event in which beings as such and as a whole are enabled to make a difference for us."[13] Moving beyond the understanding of beings as mere material on hand to be utilized with maximum efficiency and optimally exploited requires a crucial shift in our understanding of how beings as a whole and as such show up for us, which requires a new openness to the giving of being, that is, to be-ing. Being open to new ways in which entities appear allows us to be open to the question of being, which, as we have seen, Heidegger thinks has been forgotten.[14] Allowing for this openness to occur is key in moving away from the pillaging and laying to waste of the planet or the "regulating of the desolate as such."

Just as one cannot understand being without understanding its relation to beings, one cannot understand be-ing without knowing its relation to being. Since Heidegger is attempting to move beyond metaphysics, one might think that he would completely disavow speaking of being and exclusively focus on be-ing considering the fact that Heidegger comes to recognize a metaphysical connotation to being. However, in *Contributions to Philosophy*, Heidegger does not simply discard the notion of *Sein* (being) and replace it with *Seyn* (be-ing). Rather, as Polt notes, both play a role at this juncture of his path of thinking. While be-ing is "the *giving* of the being of beings,"[15] being is "the significance of beings."[16] Heidegger himself states that "being and be-ing is the same and yet fundamentally different"[17] in this work, and he calls be-ing "the hidden reign of the origin of the truth of beings as such."[18] Since he understands truth in terms of unconcealment, we can agree with Polt that be-ing has to do with the giving of the unconcealment of entities.[19] In

L revealing the truth of entities

we understand things as "Beings" [handwritten annotation]

other words, be-ing is that from which being is given. Being, on the other hand, can be understood as what *is*.[20] Being is the way in which entities are understood or, in Polt's words, "the signification of beings."

As we have seen, in the ancient Greek world, the being of an entity lies in its coming to a stand on its own, in the medieval epoch, the being of an entity lies in its being created by God, et cetera. We have yet to see what the being of entities may look like in the new beginning. What is clear, however, is that Heidegger is attempting to get away from the idea that beings are simply there to be utilized as resources for humans. I think the best way to approach what the being of entities may look like in this new beginning lies in the following passage wherein Heidegger juxtaposes the two beginnings: "In all variations and secularizations of Western metaphysics, one again recognizes that being is at the service of beings. . . . But in the other beginning beings are such that they also carry the clearing into which they are placed, which holds sway as clearing for self-sheltering and concealing, i.e., for be-ing as enowning [*Ereignis*]."[21] First, what does it mean to say that being is at the service of beings? For Heidegger, this means that entities are decisively taken for what they are (or, more appropriately, as *what we have come to take them to be*) without questioning taking them in other ways. We simply accept the everyday interpretations of beings without venturing to question them. Eventually, this leads to a leveling of all of reality since only one interpretation of beings reigns. As we noted, this type of leveling was Heidegger's main argument against the contemporary age of modern technology wherein everything is seen as mere energy on hand to be manipulated and optimally utilized. What Heidegger is striving for in the new beginning is a time in which humans are open to the different ways in which entities reveal themselves. In examining the quote, we see that Heidegger speaks of beings carrying a clearing with them in the new beginning. As Polt notes, the clearing [*Lichtung*] is the place wherein "entities as such can make sense to us."[22] Heidegger states that human beings stand in a clearing wherein things can show up *as* such-and-such for us. When there is a monolithic, one-dimensional understanding of beings that prevails, we are no longer heeding the fact that entities can reveal themselves in different ways that may be more natural or appropriate and are therefore not open to the clearing. Heidegger is hoping to show that entities need not be taken decisively in one specific way since there are innumerable ways in which beings can show up to us as meaningful.[23] Indeed, one of the goals in the new beginning is to get humans to be open to the clearing wherein things light up in different ways than the preset interpretations that have already flourished.

At the same time, however, it is not as though humans are supposed to place a haphazard interpretation on beings in any way they deem to be fitting. Humans do not decide what an interpretation of beings should be according to their own caprice. Heidegger states, "be-ing is nothing human and no human product."[24] In other words, the giving of the signification of beings is not something that humans posit; rather it is something that humans should be open to and respond to in accordance with its essential unfolding. This is the crucial aspect of Heidegger's "great turning around" in the new beginning wherein "beings are not grounded in terms of human being, but rather human being is grounded in terms of be-ing."[25] We are to respond to the various ways in which entities come to presence and place an appropriate interpretation on them while still realizing that this interpretation is never final, since there may be more appropriate ways in which to take entities in the future given the facticity of human beings. The goal is to stay true to the things themselves as they essentially unfold, and since Heidegger thinks that all natural beings are inexhaustibly complex, this requires a commitment to being open to the new ways in which entities reveal themselves. This commitment entails a flexible deference to the things themselves, which is in line with Heidegger's commitment to phenomenology. Heidegger argues that things "stand in different truths"[26] depending on one's perspective, and the key is to continually broaden one's perspective in order to be open to the different truths that adhere in any given entity.

The interpretations that are true to the things themselves are proper and appropriate, while the interpretations that are haphazardly applied and considered final are inappropriate. One must attune oneself to the ways in which entities essentially unfold and provide an interpretation that is fitting. Julian Young provides a suitable analogy of how to provide fitting interpretations of entities as they essentially are in his discussion of how this is akin to the performance of a great artwork. He states, "Though there is no definitive performance of a Beethoven symphony—great art, as great, is too multifaceted for that—the work nonetheless imposes limits outside which a performance is no longer a performance of that work but rather its violation."[27] In performing a great work of art, one is to respect the work as it essentially unfolds and do whatever one can to bring forth the multifaceted aspects of the work, knowing full well that one can never provide the perfect performance due to the inherent depth of the work. Those who simply ignore the inner workings of a Beethoven piece and go in their own direction are violating this principle. In a similar fashion, any interpretation of a natural entity should respect the essential unfolding that occurs from the entity itself. At the same time, since things always "stand in different truths" depending on one's perspective, one should never consider one's interpretation to be final, since there are always new ways in which to interpret entities that may be more appropriate in the future. The key is to always remain open to different interpretations of beings, thereby avoiding the sort of leveling effect that has occurred in the contemporary period. Before we can discuss what sorts of more appropriate ways in which to take entities might look like, we need to get a grasp as to how this shift could take place. How can we initiate a post-metaphysical understanding of reality that Heidegger speaks of when speaking of this new beginning?

EREIGNIS

In order to approach an answer to this question, we need to get some sense as to what Heidegger means by the term *das Ereignis*. Heidegger states that "what we experience in enframing as the constellation of being and man through the modern world of technology is a prelude to what is called *Ereignis*."[28] Here, we can see that Heidegger views *Ereignis* as an event that is to follow enframing. Though Heidegger does not explicitly define what this term means, it is clear that he considers it a guideword of his thought in various points of his life.[29] In fact, this term plays an essential role in Heidegger's early lectures from 1919 up to his latest works before his death, even though there are periods in his thought in which the word does not appear at all.[30] Our task is to piece together what Heidegger might mean by this term.

Ereignis has been variously translated into English by Western scholars of Heidegger. Among the most common translations are "event of appropriation," "appropriating event," "appropriation," "propriating," "enowning," "enownment," "the occurrence of owning," or simply "event."[31] We will opt to keep the term untranslated since Heidegger himself states that "it can no more be translated than the Greek λόγος or the Chinese *Dào*."[32] Just as Western commentators on the Chinese *Dào* often prefer to leave the term untranslated due to its inherent richness, I believe *Ereignis* should be left untranslated so as to avoid any unintended connotations. Guignon notes that *Ereignis* commonly means "event" in German but is "tied to the idea of 'ownness' or 'appropriation' (*eigen*), and so [suggests] 'an event of coming-into-its-own.'"[33] As is often the case, Heidegger utilizes a common word but gives it a different meaning in the context of his own thought. Heidegger himself does not offer a simplistic definition of the term, but rather provides several different ways of speaking about *Ereignis* throughout his thinking.

Polt notes that this term takes on various meanings in different points of Heidegger's corpus, but the one that is most relevant for our purposes comes from his writings in *Contributions to Philosophy* from the late 1930s wherein Heidegger is attempting to glimpse what the new beginning could look like. Polt states, "In 1936–8 [*Ereignis*] means, roughly, the possible happening in which a new dwelling may be founded: a place and age in which a people could cultivate significance."[34] The significance to be cultivated is one that gets away from the current essential unfolding of enframing that "places everything outside its own nature"[35] by subsuming everything into the standing-reserve and thereby restricting it to be revealed as merely a part of the boundless grid of energy sources. With *Ereignis*, Heidegger is attempting to open up a space in which a new, more fitting, sort of revealing may flourish. He states:

> In *Er-eignis* the possibility arises that it may overcome the mere dominance of enframing and become a more original appropriating. Such a transformation of enframing into *Er-eignis*, by virtue of that event, would bring the appropriate recovery—appropriate, hence never to be produced by man alone—of the world of technology from its dominance back to servitude in the realm by which man reaches more truly into *das Er-eignis*.[36]

In *Ereignis*, one is open to the ways in which entities come to presence on their own terms and responds to their various manifestations deferentially. Heidegger sometimes speaks of this transformation from positing what it means for a being to be in being to responding to be-ing as a *recovery* or a *saving* of beings. For instance, he states, "a *saving* [*Rettung*] of beings [is possible] *only out of the deepest* ground of be-ing itself."[37] This engagement with be-ing itself wherein a new understanding of beings as such and as a whole comes about is referred to as *Ereignis*. For Heidegger, " 'to save' is to fetch something home into its essential unfolding, in order to bring the essential unfolding for the first time into genuine appearing."[38] Heidegger's idea of saving beings has to do with allowing them to essentially unfold as they are and not apply some restrictive theoretical lens on them. In other words, the aim is to open up new ways of understanding entities that are appropriate to their own natures. Rather than seeing everything as spatiotemporal masses as we did in the early modern epoch or as units of the standing-reserve as we have come to do in the contemporary period, the goal is to open up a space wherein new understandings of entities can appear. Echoing Guignon's discussion of *Ereignis*, Polt notes, "*Er-eignis* is echoed in *sich ereignet* ['comes into its own']."[39] By allowing entities to unfold on their own terms, one is restoring their own genuine being. The interpretation of entities that comes out of this restoration is an outcome of *Ereignis*. Heidegger believes that in and through *Ereignis*, "man and Being reach each other in their nature, achieve their active nature by losing those qualities with which metaphysics has endowed them."[40] We will have to look more closely at *Contributions to Philosophy* to see what Heidegger means by this, and how he views *Ereignis* as an overcoming of metaphysics.

First, let us look at Heidegger's claim that *Ereignis* is "be-ing in thinking."[41] We have seen that be-ing is Heidegger's nonmetaphysical term for the giving of being, which we understand (roughly) as significance. As noted, Heidegger explicitly tries to distance *Ereignis* from metaphysical thinking, especially the type found in the modern epoch. For instance, he states, "It is no longer a case of talking 'about' something and representing something objective, but rather of being owned over into Er-eignis [*dem Er-eignis übereignet zu werden*]."[42] Heidegger not only aims to get out of "the usual tracks of representing"[43] that typified the early modern epoch but also to get away from the idea that everything should only be understood through the lens of enframing. To a certain extent, Heidegger is trying to get away from the idea that we need to apply any lens at all to our understanding of beings, though he realizes that our understandings are always culturally and historically influenced. For instance, even in speaking of *Ereignis*, he notes that "whatever and however we try to think, we think within the sphere of tradition."[44] It seems that the goal is to recognize that one's thoughts are infused by historical and cultural ways of thinking, but to nevertheless attempt to get away from the sort of restrictive theoretical lenses that have typified the Western tradition.

Heidegger argues that *Ereignis* is a more appropriate sort of revealing than what has occurred in previous epochs because it not only allows entities to unfold as they essentially are, but it also allows human beings to become what they essentially are as well. Let us begin with the first aspect of this, which regards the essential unfolding of beings. We noted in the previous chapter that all entities come to be seen as part of a vast array of energy sources with the onset of enframing. Heidegger claims that as everything comes to be seen as aspects of the giant energy grid, things lose any sense of uniqueness from one another. As Heidegger says, with the onset of enframing, "it is no longer important *what* each being *is*, *how* it shows itself."[45] Indeed, in the contemporary period, "Nature is set up by the human, halted by him, so that it may be accountable to him and his plans for it."[46] One of the goals of *Ereignis* is to allow beings to undergo a restoration and be understood in a way that respects how they essentially unfold.[47] Heidegger is trying to rekindle the ancient Greek idea that entities should be understood as self-emerging and self-standing, though he knows we cannot simply reinstitute an ancient Greek understanding of things and therefore calls for a postmetaphysical revealing of entities. In speaking of Heidegger's project in his later thought, Hans-Georg Gadamer, Heidegger's greatest student, states that the onset of the age of modern technology negates the "standing-in-itself of beings and lead[s] to a total leveling of them. A complete objectification of this kind would no longer represent beings that stand in their own being. Rather, it would represent nothing more than our opportunity for using beings, and what would manifest would be the will that seizes upon and dominates things."[48] He goes on to argue that a goal of Heidegger's later thought is to restore an inner fullness of being to beings, since the contemporary understanding no longer respects the ways in which entities come to presence on their own terms.

Heidegger tries to make this point by juxtaposing how natural entities unfold on their own terms and how they unfold in the age of modern technology. Consider this passage: "The birch tree never oversteps its possibility. The colony of bees dwells in its possibility. It is first the will which arranges itself everywhere in technology that devours the earth in the exhaustion and consumption and change of what is artificial. *Technology drives the earth beyond the developed sphere of its possibility.*"[49] Whereas birch trees and bee colonies remain within their possibilities as they essentially unfold on their own terms (i.e., birch trees can grow to a certain height and the bee colonies only act in certain manners in accordance with their natures), entities within the contemporary period seen as merely a part of the giant energy grid lose any sense of self-standing and lose any sense of limits or boundaries. As the emphasis becomes efficiency and optimal use of resources, we find things like genetically modified foods that could have never existed naturally and the genetically engineered trees that we spoke of in the last chapter.[50] In short, entities are either pushed beyond their natural limits or we find a way of creating entities that will meet our needs when natural beings are unable to do so. Heidegger sometimes speaks in terms of the will, the gigantic, or enframing as such when speaking of the emphasis on efficiency and optimization in the modern technological age and the unwillingness to recognize the limits of things, but all of these terms express an inappropriate sense of unmitigated domination. Here, "the earth and its atmosphere become raw material"[51] as "technological dominion spreads itself over the earth ever more quickly, ruthlessly, and completely."[52] The goal, I believe, is to reinstate an understanding of things that is truer to their self-standing. This is true for both natural beings and human beings. Natural beings are to be understood according to their own limits, and human beings are to become who they essentially are as well, which is not the lords of the earth that they have become in the contemporary period, but rather the shepherds of being, which means the ones who bring forth interpretations of entities in accordance with their essential or *natural* unfolding.[53] A different sort of comportment towards natural beings and the natural world as such is required to enact this shift. On my interpretation, *Ereignis* is the "activity" of opening up to the ways in which entities come to presence on their own terms, and once this event occurs, we are able to initiate a new sort of human comportment towards, or more appropriately, *with*, nature.

One initial obstacle with Heidegger's later thought is that he does not explicitly tell us how to enact *Ereignis*. In fact, he states:

No one can know whether and when and where and how this step of thinking will develop into a proper (needed in *Ereignis*) path and way and road-building.

Instead, the rule of metaphysics may rather entrench itself, in the shape of modern technology with its developments rushing along boundlessly. Or, everything that results by way of the step back may merely be exploited and absorbed by metaphysics in its own way.[54]

Since Heidegger doesn't think that this shift from enframing to *Ereignis* is something that humans can willfully bring about, Thomas Sheehan states that he doesn't leave us much hope for a bright future for the planet and the human place within it. He states, "If one follows Heidegger's thinking . . . consistently, there is . . . no hope for a new age when the balance might shift back in favor of nature."[55] While Sheehan's point should be noted, the fact that Heidegger himself does not provide clear guidance as to how to enact *Ereignis* does not preclude us from gaining a sense as to what *Ereignis* in practice would entail. Heidegger does offer a vision of a more appropriate way in which to understand the world around us and comport ourselves toward nature in his later thoughts on freedom, letting beings be, and dwelling. We must therefore understand these concepts in order to determine what a practical version of *Ereignis* might look like.

FREEDOM, LETTING BE, AND DWELLING

Heidegger's notions of letting beings be [*Gelassenheit*] and freedom [*Freiheit*] are his attempts to speak about what a new sort of comportment could look like. When letting be and freedom are accomplished, we no longer understand everything in terms of human interests and begin to understand things on their own terms. Heidegger states, "as soon as we are capable of . . . letting something be in that into which—as into its own essential unfolding—it is let, then we are truly free. Freedom rests in being able to let, not in ordering and dominating."[56] Whereas enframing "demands that nature be orderable as standing-reserve"[57] and therefore involves a domineering attitude, letting beings be takes a step back and allows entities to unfold in their own particular and proper manners. Heidegger defines letting a being be as "letting something essentially unfold in its provenance."[58] Although we tend to think of letting something be as a passive attitude of indifference, Heidegger stresses that letting be is not a matter of simply stepping back and passively allowing beings to unfold, since letting be is not tantamount to some sort of withdrawal from interaction with beings. In fact, he states that it lies "outside the distinction between activity and passivity . . . because it does not belong to the domain of the will."[59] The goal is to stop thinking in terms of willing, manipulation, or domination, and start thinking in terms of cultivation and saving. Heidegger says that to save means "to loose[n], to emancipate, to free, to spare and husband, to harbor protectingly, to take under one's care, to keep safe."[60] The idea of letting be, which is a sort of saving, is a matter of emancipating things from being understood in the inappropriate sense of standing-reserve and allowing for or letting a more appropriate way of manifestation flourish that is truer to the ways in which entities reveal themselves.

As can be glimpsed from the previous passages, freedom has to do with the idea of saving and is in line with letting be. Though we tend to think of having freedom along the lines of being able to do whatever we want, Heidegger argues that this sense of freedom is not the original sense since it is caught up with the ideas of willing and dominating that have come to take on an unprecedented prominence in the contemporary period.[61] Just as letting be is beyond the sphere of activity and passivity and the realm of the will, Heidegger's notion of freedom is outside these concepts, and he argues that his conception of freedom is a more appropriate sense than the "do as one wishes" sort of freedom that is commonly associated with the term. Guignon provides a nice passage on Heidegger's notion of freedom and its relation to letting be in his discussion of the early Heidegger:

> Freeing up or letting be requires that we resist our common tendency to impose onto things a prior grid of interpretation designed to make them fit our antecedent expectations. In freeing, we give things the breathing room they need to unfold in their own proper way, to "essence" (in Heidegger's verbal use of the word *wesen*) without foisting on them an interpretive schema determined by our interests and projects.[62]

This idea of freeing up and giving things breathing room links up with the German word *das Freie*, which has the connotation of open air or open space.[63] By freeing up entities from the restrictive theoretical lens that has been applied in the age of modern technology, humans begin to engage in letting beings be. Heidegger states, "Freedom for what is opened up in an open region lets beings be the beings they are. Freedom now reveals itself as letting beings be."[64] Heidegger clearly understands freedom and letting be on the same terms, and he eventually understands them in the positive sense of preserving [*schonen*] in his late essay, "Building, Dwelling, Thinking." Here, Heidegger states, "To free actually means to preserve. The preserving itself consists not only in the fact that we do not harm the one we preserve. Real preserving is something *positive* and takes place when we leave something beforehand in its own essential unfolding, when we return it specifically to its essential being."[65] Heidegger's notion of preserving is not a matter of standing back and leaving oneself unattached to things. Rather, the idea is to engage with things and allow them to show up as the things that they are.

Bruce Foltz provides a nice commentary on what *schonen* means in the sense that Heidegger intends it in the following passage: "The German *schonen* does not mean to refrain from using something or to set it aside, but to use it in such a way that harm is not inflicted upon it; used reflexively or with regard to things, it means 'to look after' in the sense that one 'looks after one's health.'"⁶⁶ Just as one does not care for one's health by neglecting it or remaining unattached to it, but rather by paying attention to what goes into one's body and how the body responds to it, genuine preserving is a matter of living on the earth in a way that does not neglect the ways in which things unfold on their own terms and what beings require to reach their ideal state. Just as the good gardener is attentive to what his or her plants need to reach their fruition and blossom in a healthy manner, those who preserve are attentive to the ways in which entities unfold and let beings do so on their own terms. This, to Heidegger, is the way in which human beings should live. He calls this sort of living "dwelling" [*wohnen*]. Heidegger states, "To dwell . . . means to remain at peace within the free, the preserve, the free sphere that safeguards each thing in its essential unfolding. *The fundamental character of dwelling is this preserving.*"⁶⁷ Humans are to live in a way that respects the natures of things. Again, Heidegger links this up with saving. He states, "Mortals dwell in that they save the earth . . . To save properly means to set something free into its own essential unfolding. To save the earth is more than to exploit it or even wear it out. Saving the earth does not master the earth and does not subjugate it, which is merely one step from boundless spoliation."⁶⁸ Dwelling is a way of living on the earth that does not master or dominate it. The only way in which to do this is to respect the ways in which beings essentially are. In respecting the natural ways in which entities unfold, one becomes closer to treating things in a manner that is fitting towards them. Instead of viewing forests as merely a giant inventory of timber, for instance, one sees the forests as a habitat for animals, a boon for the soil, and a product of innumerable processes of nature. When one is able to see the forests in this fashion, one has reached the first step towards living in a way that respects the forests as what they are, rather than simply treating them as a mere resource as we have come to be accustomed to in the contemporary period.

We can now see the relation between viewing natural beings as they truly are and how it connects with dwelling in regard to specific natural entities such as forests. The question remains as to what dwelling might actually consist in considering the current state of things. Keeping in mind the fact that we are in the age of modern technology, what would a world in which people have learned to dwell actually look like? I think that part of the answer lies in Heidegger's idea that building belongs to dwelling. The ways in which we create buildings and technological devices can either allow the possibility for dwelling or can stifle it. In his essay, "Building, Dwelling, Thinking," Heidegger offers an example of the sort of building that is in accordance with dwelling with his description of an old bridge. He states, "The bridge lets the stream run its course and at the same time grants mortals their way, so that they may come and go from shore to shore."[69] Heidegger is envisioning a way of living in the world that respects the ways of nature and allows natural beings to run their own course rather than mastering over them. For Heidegger, an old bridge allows for dwelling. In "The Question Concerning Technology," Heidegger tells us how this contrasts with the way in which humans live in the contemporary period wherein enframing rules in speaking of the hydroelectric plant. He states, "The hydroelectric plant is not built into the Rhine River as was the old wooden bridge that joined bank with bank for hundreds of years. Rather the river is dammed up into the power plant. What the river is now, namely a water power supplier, derives from out of the essence of the power station."[70] Whereas the hydroelectric plant treats the river as merely a supply of energy to be exploited with maximum efficiency, the bridge respects the river as a river and allows it to flow on its own terms. In this way, the bridge allows for an appropriate relation to nature. In coming across an old bridge that joins two banks, one can still respect the banks *as* banks and the river *as* river, whereas in coming across a hydroelectric plant, one gets the impression that the river is simply there to supply energy to the plant. In this way, the hydroelectric plant does not let beings be the beings that they are in the way that the bridge does. Moreover, since the energy that is supplied to the plant is ultimately utilized to quench human interests, buildings like the hydroelectric plant only reinforce the idea that nature is something to be mastered or conquered by humans and manipulated to our interests. The bridge, on the other hand, does not reinforce this attitude since it is built into the land and allows the landscape to be what it is, as it is, rather than transforming it into something alien and aligning it to meet our own interests.

We should be quick to point out that Heidegger is not saying that we must completely refrain from utilizing natural entities as resources altogether. Rather, he is simply arguing against viewing them *merely* as resources. In order to make this point clear, he speaks of an old windmill that clearly turns the wind into power but still allows the wind to be wind.[71] While the hydroelectric plant dams the water and forces it to acquiesce to the interests of humans without respecting its natural flow, thereby treating it as a mere resource, the old windmill allows humans to utilize the wind as an energy resource without manipulating the flow of the wind. As Heidegger says, "the sails . . . are left entirely to the wind's blowing."[72] Instead of challenging the wind to provide energy for humans in a manner similar to the way in which the hydroelectric plant challenges the water, the old windmill simply uses the natural energy that is imminent within the wind for power. The whole idea is to respect entities on their own terms rather than disregarding the ways in which they naturally unfold. In dwelling, one respects the ways in which beings naturally unfold and still uses them as resources.

Another example that Heidegger utilizes comes in the field of woodworking. He states, "If [one] is to become a true cabinetmaker, he makes himself answer and respond to the shapes slumbering within wood—to wood as it enters into man's dwelling with all the hidden riches of its nature."[73] A good cabinetmaker knows the shapes and contours hidden inside the wood and makes cabinets in accordance with these natural grains, rather than going against them or ignoring them altogether. In this way, the cabinetmaker respects the essential unfolding of the tree and utilizes it at the same time. On a wider scale, a good woodworker knows that cedar is much more malleable than oak and, therefore, utilizes the softer cedar for projects that call for more flexibility such as a decorative gazebo. If a project calls for more durability (as in, say, a bookcase), a harder wood like oak is the more appropriate choice. It is important to point out that it is not simply a matter of efficiency (in the sense of what is fastest, cheapest, and easiest) in one's choice of wood; rather, it is a matter of what is most *fitting* for the project at hand, given the wood's typical natural constitution, the unique inhering properties of the particular piece of timber itself, and the particular project that one has before oneself. One can see how this is very different from simply viewing forests as a conglomerate of timber to be maximally utilized, as it is in the age of modern technology. In the words of Heidegger, "Where in the manipulations of the industrial worker is there any relatedness to such things as the shapes slumbering within wood?"[74] The modern lumber industry does not heed the hidden shapes of the wood but rather treats the forest as a giant array of resources to be utilized with maximum efficiency. For the modern industrial worker, "the wood is a forest of timber."[75]

Speaking broadly, the notion of dwelling entails living within the earth rather than mastering over the earth. As Remmon Barbaza notes, Heidegger's notion of dwelling gives us a hint as to the relation that Heidegger may see in the new beginning with the first beginning that occurred in ancient Greece. He states, "To dwell poetically is to live in a way that does not encroach on the bringing-forth of *phusis* but that takes part in this very bringing-forth."[76] As we saw earlier, the ancient Greeks understood φύσις as self-emerging. Though the pre-Socratics understood being as φύσις, the Western metaphysical tradition eventually restricted its understanding of being to οὐσία, which eventually led to viewing beings as standing-reserve. Heidegger's new beginning involves some sort of reinstatement of allowing things to emerge on their own terms and therefore involves a sense of self-emergence and self-standing as we saw in the ancient Greek epoch. As we have seen, this does not necessarily mean that we must step back and completely refrain from utilizing natural entities. Rather, dwelling in the new beginning would involve utilizing resources without overly exploiting them.

Allowing entities to be what they are, thereby attaining freedom, allows one to encounter entities as *things*. Heidegger's mature thinking on what it means to be a thing comes in his 1950 lecture, "The Thing." Here, he states that a jug of wine, when properly used, is a thing. Speaking of when one pours a libation as a sacrifice to the gods, he states, "To pour a gush, when it is achieved in its essence, thought through with sufficient generosity, and genuinely uttered, is to donate, to offer sacrifice, and hence to give. It is only for this reason that the pouring of the gush, once its nature withers, can become a mere pouring in and pouring out, until it finally decays into the dispensing of liquor at the bar."[77] In ancient Greece, wine was closely linked to sacrifice and celebration. The outpouring of wine was often at a significant event and was usually done at a ceremony to bless an occasion such as a wedding or at a festival to mark a new season. An important aspect of such sacrifices is that they were often done at social gatherings, and Heidegger thinks that it is at such occasions that things can properly *be* things. A genuine offering in this context recognizes a significant event and highlights the interconnectedness among things. Heidegger calls this a moment of gathering. He states, "The thing things. Thinging gathers. . . . The jug's essential nature . . . is what we call *thing*."[78] While it may seem foreign to American ears to say "the thing things," turning a noun into a verb is common in the German language. For Heidegger, this feature of the German language is particularly useful because he understands things as entities essentially interlinked with other things rather than as independent, static substances. In fact, Heidegger says that things are entities that essentially gather.[79] To understand "thinging," one must understand the connection Heidegger sees between things and gathering. If we think of the pouring of a libation at a wedding ceremony, one can see this occasion as a moment of gathering. The two lives that are united together have been formed by their relationships with the family and friends who have joined them to celebrate. Above and beyond these human relations are the relations between the thinging of the jug and the other events that were necessary for this occasion. Heidegger calls the interrelation of these events the fourfold [*das Geviert*], which consists of earth, sky, mortals, and the gods. The earth forms the grapes through nourishment; the sky provides sunlight and water; mortals not only join to celebrate but have crafted the grapes into wine and molded the jug as a proper vessel; and the gods are asked to bless the occasion as a sacrificial libation is made to them. In the true thinging of the thing, all of these relations come forth, and one is mindful of them if one is to freely embrace the moment. If one attains a respective mindfulness of the interrelatedness of the entities that make up the event, in this case a wedding, one respects the things involved in the occasion. In *dwelling on* this interrelatedness, one *dwells in* the moment of gathering.

Heidegger notes that things can decay into mindless entities to consume, which is why he mentions the mere dispensing of liquor at a bar. If we juxtapose the potency of meaning that accompanies the pouring of a libation at a wedding with the mindless consumption of a solitary man's fifth drink of whiskey at a dingy bar, we can see a vast difference in the events that take place. While the ceremony gathers events from the past and signals a commitment amongst the man and wife in the future, the pouring of the fifth whiskey to the man who eagerly escapes his sober existence does not allow for thinging, since the gathering of entities that allowed for this moment is taken for granted or ignored completely. The whiskey in this instance becomes merely an entity to consume rather than a thing of this world, a world that Heidegger comes to understand as the interplay among earth, sky, mortals, and gods.[80]

Those who attain freedom and allow things to be things become those who dwell. Heidegger states, "The way in which you are and I am, the manner in which we humans *are* on the earth, is . . . dwelling. To be a human being means to be on the earth as a mortal. It means to dwell."[81] In other words, the proper *being* of human beings lies in dwelling. Those who dwell appreciate the interconnectedness of things around them by being mindful of their origins and proper unfolding. It does not necessarily take a special occasion like a wedding in which the gathering is charged with meaning to allow for dwelling. Rather, as Heidegger points out, dwelling is accomplished whenever one lets things be the things that they are, which is accomplished when entities are accepted in accordance with their proper limits. Heidegger invokes the Greek word πέρας [*peras*], which can be translated as "end," "limit," or "boundary"[82] to make this point. He states, "a boundary is not that at which something stops but, as the Greeks recognized, the boundary is that from which something *begins its essential unfolding*."[83] We can think of πέρας as the range of possibilities that naturally inhere in an entity. All natural beings have appropriate limits or boundaries that need to be acknowledged and accepted in order to respect them on their own terms. If we revisit our woodworking example from earlier, we can say that the true craftsman who has perfected the art of woodworking respects the inhering possibilities in the woods themselves, while the unskilled novice may just hack away at the wood without any regard for what the wood is in its nature. The skilled craftsman is at home with the inhering possibilities of the wood and utilizes them in his craft to his advantage, while the novice has yet to build this sort of affinity with the wood, and is therefore less adept at crafting an item that is fitting of its nature.

Along with a respectful deference to things as they are in themselves, dwelling entails a mindful circumspective eye towards the interrelatedness of things. A woodworker, for instance, would respect all the years of growth that went into making the wood what it is today, and the intricacies that make this particular piece of wood unique. In crafting the item that he is to create, he is respectful of everything that has gone into producing the piece and will therefore reflect on the appropriate ways to utilize the wood before attempting the mold it into a product that is fitting for humans to use. This understanding of what the wood *is*, which includes where it comes from, how it has gotten there, and what it should be used for, allows for an appreciation of the material, and helps to close off the possibility that the wood will be mindlessly exploited. Such an appreciation is seen in the environmental philosophical classic, *A Sand County Almanac*, when Leopold recalls his days of woodworking in his youth: "We sensed that [the] piles of sawdust were something more than wood: that they were the integrated transect of a century; that our saw was biting its way, stroke by stroke, decade by decade, into the chronology of a lifetime, written in concentric annual rings of good oak."[84] Leopold's ecological consciousness is shown by his understanding of the years of development that goes into a healthy tree. By being mindful of this natural development, one is less likely to mindlessly exploit the tree in the name of economic development.

An appropriate question at this point might be how one accomplishes this mindful dwelling in one's everyday life. Heidegger provides the following answer: "When and in what way do things appear as things? They do not appear *by means of* human making. But neither do they appear without the vigilance of mortals. The first step toward such vigilance is the step back from the thinking that merely represents—that is, explains—to the thinking that responds and recalls."[85] This sort of thinking requires a respectful responsiveness to things as they show themselves and a reflective capacity to appreciate things in their contextual relationships with other entities. In a public lecture in 1955 in which he commemorated the posthumous birthday of Conradin Kreutzer, a German composer from his hometown, Heidegger gives us a glimpse as to what this sort of thinking that responds and recalls looks like. Here, he laments the pervasive thoughtlessness that all too often occurs in today's world, stating that "one gathering follows on the heels of another,"[86] implying that such "gatherings" are not *gatherings* at all since a respectful mindfulness of the occasion is lacking. In an attempt to truly commemorate the event, Heidegger states, "It is enough if we dwell on what lies close and meditate on what is closest; upon that which concerns us, each one of us, here and now; here, on this patch of home ground; now, in the present hour of history."[87] He goes on to reflect on the significance of this event by speaking of the relationship between humans and their homeland [*Heimat*]. At such an occasion, it is appropriate to reflect on how one's geographical roots shape humans into the persons that they become, and how a notable life, in this case the life of Conradin Kreutzer, can teach us how to live our own lives. An important aspect of dwelling that comes through in this passage is

that dwelling involves *dwelling on* an event in its situational context. The com-
memoration, as a moment of gathering, attains the status of a significant event
if there is a thoughtful reflection involved wherein one respects its importance.
The more we can dwell on events such as this moment of gathering or on things
as they are in themselves, the more we are able to attain dwelling among things.

The question is what an everyday existence would look like for someone
who dwells. One potential answer to this question could be seen in looking at
Heidegger's everyday existence in his days spent in his hut at Todtnauberg in
the mountains of Germany's Black Forest. Though Heidegger did own a house
in the city, he also owned a small hut where he spent his time writing in solitude. Here, Heidegger learned to live with the land and even felt a strong connection to the landscape, its people, and what was most important to him: his
work. As Adam Sharr notes in his book, *Heidegger's Hut*, "Heidegger thought
and wrote at the hut over five decades, often alone, claiming an emotional and
intellectual intimacy with the building, its surroundings, and its seasons."[88]
When Heidegger was offered a professorship at the University of Berlin, which
is perhaps the most prestigious philosophy position in all of Germany, he
refused, citing an "inner relationship of [his] own work to the Black Forest and
its people."[89] Heidegger explains the intimate connection between the land and
his work as follows:

> Strictly speaking I myself never observe the landscape. I experience its hourly
> changes, day and night, in the great comings and goings of the seasons. The
> gravity of the mountains and the hardness of their primeval rock, the slow and
> deliberate growth of the fir-trees, the brilliant, simple splendor of the meadows
> in bloom, the rush of the mountain brook in the long autumn night, the stern
> simplicity of the flatlands covered with snow—all of this moves and flows
> through and penetrates daily existence up there, and not in forced moments of
> "aesthetic" immersion or artificial empathy, but only when one's existence
> stands in its work. It is the work alone that opens up space for the reality that is
> these mountains. The course of the work remains embedded in what happens in
> the region.[90]

Clearly, Heidegger felt a deep connection to his work and the place in which
it was carried out. I think the most important part of this passage for our
purposes lies in how much Heidegger viewed his daily existence as immersed
in the changing of the seasons and nature's own course. Instead of viewing
his environmental surrounding as an aesthetically pleasing landscape or a
recreational opportunity and thereby merely subsuming it in terms of his own
interests, Heidegger lives *within* the environment and *through* the environment in a way that is respectful of it. Moreover, Heidegger finds inspiration
from the world around him in regard to his work. Of course, this is not to say
that Heidegger did not use the environment around him. He had a well from

which he fetched his water, obtained his firewood from the surrounding trees for warmth and cooking, utilized the winds to dry his clothing, and enjoyed skiing on the slopes of the mountains.[91] Heidegger clearly utilized the environment around him for resources and for recreational activity. However, his simple use of the land did not take away from his overarching respect for it. During his days spent at his cottage, Heidegger learned to dwell upon and within the earth rather than rule over it.

BECOMING WHAT WE ESSENTIALLY ARE

Heidegger says that "[mortals] *must ever learn to dwell.*"[92] The question that confronts us is how we can undergo such a radical change in our being-in-the-world. How can we dwell upon the earth and get away from viewing everything in terms of resources to be utilized with maximum efficiency? I believe Heidegger's answer lies in this passage: "*Before* considering the question that is seemingly always the most immediate one and the only urgent one, What shall we do? We ponder this: *How must we think?*"[93] According to Heidegger, what it means to be fully human is to engage in thinking. He states, "man still is the being who *is* insofar as he thinks."[94] What this means is that the *being* of human beings lies in their ability to think. Heidegger argues that a distinctive feature of contemporary humanity is the pervasive thoughtlessness that "comes and goes everywhere in today's world."[95] He states, "nowadays we take in everything in the quickest and cheapest way, only to forget it just as quickly, instantly."[96] Obviously, this is even truer today than it was when he uttered these words. With the pervasiveness of televisions, laptops, and smartphones that allow us to summon information at the touch of a button, it is easy to become dependent on technological devices for one's information. Instead of actually engaging in any particular subject, we can retrieve information from the Internet at the tip of our fingers. As we come to utilize these devices more regularly, they become a part of our everyday existence and we come to rely upon them. In relying upon such devices, however, we engage less in thinking itself and more in thoughtlessness, since we allow the technological devices to "do the thinking for us," as it were.[97] As we pointed out in the previous chapter, Heidegger does not argue against technology as such or even specific technological devices. What he argues against is becoming "so firmly shackled to these technical devices that we fall into bondage to them"[98] such that we no longer engage in thinking.

The question is what sort of thinking we should engage in. As one could likely surmise, Heidegger espouses the sort of thinking that opens up new ways of looking at things. In order to make this point, he juxtaposes calculative thinking with meditative thinking. While calculative thinking is thinking that works within the confines of what is already established, meditative thinking investigates new avenues and new ways of looking at things. Heidegger states, "Meditative thinking demands of us not to cling one-sidedly to a single idea, nor to run down a one-track course of ideas."[99] Instead, meditative thinking looks at entities from the perspective of the whole and thereby sees things in a new light. The German word translated as "meditative thinking" is *die Besin-nung*. The word *Sinn* means "meaning" and the prefix *Be-* is an intensifier that has to do with the whole.[100] So we can think of meditative thinking as thinking that has to do with the whole, rather than thinking that analyzes parts. We can think of this in terms of the deep and shallow solutions to the environmental crisis that we spoke of in chapter 2. While the shallow solutions work within the already set social, political, and cultural structures, the deeper solution results in fundamentally changing the way in which we view reality as a whole and the human place in it. Instead of thinking solely in terms of economic progress and growth, which has clearly come to be one of the most important guiding factors for our choices with the onset of the global market, the deeper solution involves taking a step back and looking at things in a different light. It involves viewing forests as habitats, water as the source of all life, and food as a resource that is limited and even scarce in many parts of the world. It involves viewing things as what they are, rather than viewing them explicitly through human interests. It involves recognizing the limits of both natural resources and the power of human beings. It involves respecting the interconnectedness of ecosystemic relations and the human reliance on healthy ecosystems. This begins with a step in thinking rather than doing.

In the public address of 1955, Heidegger links up meditative thinking with letting beings be since it involves being open to different ways in which entities manifest themselves. In speaking of letting beings be, he states that it "grant[s] us the possibility of dwelling in the world in a totally different way."[101] Here, we can see the connection between thinking and dwelling. By taking a step back and letting beings be, we become capable of dwelling. Again, the emphasis is on thinking before simply doing. Heidegger once stated, "It could be that prevailing man has for centuries now acted too much and thought too little."[102] The goal is to be the beings that we essentially are, those who think, which will allow us to then act in the appropriate manners and accomplish dwelling.

Perhaps we can now begin to see the connection between our essence as human beings and overcoming the age of modern technology. In engaging in meditative thinking, we become able to look at things in new ways and perhaps find more appropriate ways in which to view beings. Heidegger links this up to overcoming enframing in the following passage: "In order that man in his essence may become attentive to the essential unfolding of technology [i.e., enframing], and in order that there may be found an essential relationship between technology and man in respect to their essence, modern man must first and above all find his way back into the full breadth of the space proper to his essence."[103] This entails taking a step back and thinking about the ways in which one is changing the landscape of both the world and humanity's place within it. Humans have come to understand themselves to be the lords of nature and everything in it, but this is not true to their essential nature. Heidegger states, "The human being is not the lord of beings. The human being is the shepherd of being."[104] Due to our capability of engaging in thinking, we are capable of opening up the signification of beings and, in doing so, we become what we essentially are. This links up with our earlier discussion of *Ereignis*. Just as *Ereignis* allows entities to essentially unfold on their own terms and thereby come into their own, humans who engage in this shift in their understanding of their place in nature by cultivating *Ereignis* and allowing things to show up as the things that they are become who they are as well. In doing so, humans come into their own, which Heidegger understands as being the shepherds of being.

If we are to place an environmental spin on meditative thinking and dwelling, we can say that a proper dictum to guide one's practice is to "think globally and act locally." Dwelling on responds to the call of "thinking globally" or thinking of beings as a whole, since it entails a reflective appreciation of what things are in their limitations and how things are essentially related to one another. One of the aspects of modern environmentalism that contemporary thinkers struggle with is that seemingly innocuous acts—one's daily commute to work by car, buying groceries from the supermarket, setting the dial of one's thermostat, et cetera—have detrimental consequences on a global scale. If we heed Heidegger's call to dwell on things before we act, we would take into consideration how our actions are related to the environmental crisis. The more we dwell on our actions and the relationships that are essentially implicated in them, the more we attain dwelling among things, which implies treating things with a respectful deference to what they are in and of themselves. And a wide-ranging knowledge of things would require one to move away from transnational corporate consumption and towards a more local approach, thereby responding to the environmentalist's call to "act locally."

Ideally, a Heideggerian environmental ethic is one in which a *responsiveness* to things as they naturally unfold opens up a *responsibility* to sustain their natural unfolding. Since Heidegger eschews ethics in the normative sense, he provides no guidance as to which natural entities do and do not deserve moral consideration. His philosophy does, however, provide the scaffolding from which to build an environmental ethic upon that goes beyond the Western metaphysical tradition. In fact, the environmentally relevant aspects of Heidegger's thought show a deep affinity with one of the earliest environmental philosophies in the world, philosophical Daoism, as Eric Sean Nelson notes:

"Daoism challenges and provides a richer alternative to the anthropocentric and instrumental tendencies of western metaphysics diagnosed so well by Heidegger, including the critiques and reversals of this tradition which remain beholden to it."[105] Our task in the next chapter will be to show the similarities between Heidegger's philosophy and philosophical Daoism with an emphasis on the environmentally relevant aspects in order to show how Heidegger cultivates a nonmetaphysical understanding of reality.

NOTES

1. Heidegger, *Contributions to Philosophy*, 129 [GA 65, 184]. I analyze Heidegger's *Seyn* as opposed to *Sein* below.
2. Heidegger, *Contributions to Philosophy*, 129 [GA 65, 184].
3. Heidegger, *The Essence of Human Freedom*, 36 [GA 31, 51].
4. Heidegger, "Overcoming Metaphysics," 90 [GA 7, 75].
5. Cf. Heidegger, *Contributions to Philosophy*, 4 [GA 65, 5].
6. Heidegger, *Contributions to Philosophy*, 5 [GA 65, 5].
7. Heidegger, *Contributions to Philosophy*, 161 [GA 65, 227].
8. As we will see later, Heidegger does not believe that humans can simply initiate this great turnaround, but must rather wait for the turnaround to occur. As to the other issue, we will see how the new beginning links up to the first beginning later in the chapter.
9. Heidegger, *Mindfulness*, 78 [GA 66, 93].
10. Heidegger, *Contributions to Philosophy*, 3 [GA 65, 3]. As Vallega-Neu points out, be-ing-historical thinking is Heidegger's way of getting away from his search for an ultimate ontological structure of being that he did in his earlier thought. She states, "Be-ing is no longer articulated, as in *Being and Time*, by means of an ontological structure which underlies history (in *Being and Time* Heidegger thinks history as being grounded in Dasein's temporality). Instead, be-ing itself opens as a historical occurrence, and thinking finds itself partaking in this occurrence" (*Heidegger's* Contributions to Philosophy, 30).
11. Heidegger, *Contributions to Philosophy*, 287 [GA 65, 408–409].
12. Vallega-Neu, *Heidegger's* Contributions to Philosophy, 7, footnote 1.
13. Polt, *The Emergency of Being*, 28–29.
14. Heidegger states, "since Plato no inquiry has been made into the *truth* of the interpretation of 'being'" (*Contributions to Philosophy*, 132 [GA 65, 188]).
15. Polt, *The Emergency of Being*, 59.
16. Polt, *The Emergency of Being*, 17. I should note that other commentators see no opposition between *Seyn* and *Sein*. For instance, Parvis Emad and Kenneth Maly, the translators of *Contributions to Philosophy*, state that Heidegger "intends no opposition" between *Seyn* and *Sein* (Introduction, xxii). However, I will argue for Polt's position.
17. Heidegger, *Contributions to Philosophy*, 120 [GA 65, 171].
18. Heidegger, *Contributions to Philosophy*, 41 [GA 65, 58].

19. Heidegger thinks that the more original sense of truth is not correspondence with reality but rather unconcealment. Cf. Heidegger, *Introduction to Metaphysics*, 211 [GA 40, 144–145], on his discussion of truth as *aletheia*. Since it is not directly relevant to our purposes, I will not discuss Heidegger's controversial conception of truth.

20. Cf. chapter 2.

21. Heidegger, *Contributions to Philosophy*, 162 [GA 65, 230] (translation modified). I will go into depth as to what *Ereignis* might mean later in the chapter.

22. Polt, *The Emergency of Being*, 168.

23. For an excellent commentary on how we should be open to the various ways in which entities manifest themselves, see Hubert L. Dreyfus's "Heidegger on the Connection between Nihilism, Art, Technology, and Politics," in *The Cambridge Companion to Heidegger*, ed. Charles Guignon (Cambridge: Cambridge University Press, 1993), 289–316.

24. Heidegger, *Contributions to Philosophy*, 187 [GA 65, 265].

25. Heidegger, *Contributions to Philosophy*, 129 [GA 65, 184].

26. Heidegger, *What Is a Thing?* 26 [GA 41, 25].

27. Julian Young, *Heidegger's Later Philosophy* (Cambridge: Cambridge University Press, 2002), 40.

28. Martin Heidegger, *Identity and Difference*, 36–37 [GA 11, 45–46] (translation modified).

29. Cf. Heidegger, *Identity and Difference*, 36 [GA 11, 45].

30. On his early works addressing *das Ereignis*, see his *Towards the Definition of Philosophy* [GA 56/57]. The later works that deal with this concept are published in the volume *Four Seminars*, trans. Andrew Mitchell and François Raffoul (Bloomington and Indianapolis: Indiana University Press, 2003) [GA 15].

31. For the various translations of *das Ereignis* and their strengths and weaknesses, see Polt, *The Emergency of Being*, 10, footnote 22.

32. Heidegger, *Identity and Difference*, 36 [GA 11, 45].

33. Guignon, "Introduction," 18.

34. Richard Polt, "*Ereignis*," in *A Companion to Heidegger*, ed. Hubert L. Dreyfus and Mark Wrathall (Malden, Mass.: Blackwell, 2005), 376.

35. Heidegger, "The Thing," 166 [GA 7, 168].

36. Heidegger, *Identity and Difference*, 37 [GA 11, 46].

37. Heidegger, *Contributions to Philosophy*, 69 [GA 65, 100].

38. Heidegger, "The Question Concerning Technology," 28 [GA 7, 29] (translation modified).

39. Polt, *The Emergency of Being*, 14.

40. Heidegger, *Identity and Difference*, 37 [GA 11, 46].

41. Heidegger, *Contributions to Philosophy*, 330 [GA 65, 470].

42. Heidegger, *Contributions to Philosophy*, 3 [GA 65, 3] (translation modified).

43. Heidegger, *Contributions to Philosophy*, 190 [GA 65, 269].

44. Heidegger, *Identity and Difference*, 41 [GA 11, 50].

45. Heidegger, *Mindfulness*, 92 [GA 66, 110].

46. Heidegger, *Country Path Conversations*, trans. Bret W. Davis (Bloomington and Indianapolis: Indiana University Press, 2010), 7 [GA 77, 12].

47. Cf. Heidegger, *Contributions to Philosophy*, 6 [GA 65, 7].

48. Hans-Georg Gadamer, "Heidegger's Later Philosophy," in *Philosophical Hermeneutics*, trans. David E. Linge (Berkeley: University of California Press, 1976), 226–227.

49. Heidegger, "Overcoming Metaphysics," 109 [GA 7, 96].

50. For an interesting take on Heidegger's thought and genetically enhanced foods, see Gregory E. Pence, "Genetically Modified Crops, Environmental Ethics, and Ecofascism," in *Designer Food: Mutant Harvest or Breadbasket of the World?* (Lanham, Md.: Rowman & Littlefield, 2002), chapter 6.

51. Heidegger, "What Are Poets For?" 111 [GA 5, 289].

52. Heidegger, "What Are Poets For?" 114 [GA 5, 292].

53. Cf. Heidegger, *Pathmarks*, 260 [GA 9, 172].

54. Heidegger, *Identity and Difference*, 72–73 [GA 11, 78].

55. Thomas Sheehan, "Nihilism: Heidegger/Jünger/Aristotle," in *Phenomenology: Japanese and American Perspectives*, ed. Burt C. Hopkins (Boston: Kluwer Academic Publishers, 2010), 297.

56. Martin Heidegger, *Country Path Conversations*, 149 [GA 77, 230].

57. Heidegger, "The Question Concerning Technology," 23 [GA 7, 24].

58. Heidegger, *Pathmarks*, 241 [GA 9, 316].

59. Heidegger, *Country Path Conversations*, 70 [GA 77, 109].

60. Martin Heidegger, "The Turning," in *The Question Concerning Technology and Other Essays*, trans. William Lovitt (New York: Harper & Row, 1977), 42 [GA 79, 172].

61. For instance, Heidegger states, "Freedom is not mere absence of constraint with respect to what we can or cannot do" in his 1930 essay, "On the Essence of Truth," in *Pathmarks*, 145 [GA 9, 189].

62. Charles Guignon, "Heidegger's Concept of Freedom, 1927-1930," in *Interpreting Heidegger: Critical Essays*, ed. Daniel O. Dahlstrom (Cambridge: Cambridge University Press, 2011), 92. I should point out that Guignon says that such freeing is "mostly passive." In his early thought, Heidegger's notion of freedom can be integrated into the schema of passivity and activity, but in his later thought he attempts to think outside these concepts altogether.

63. Cf. William Lovitt's footnote 23 in Heidegger, "The Question Concerning Technology," 25.

64. Heidegger, *Pathmarks*, 144 [GA 9, 188].

65. Martin Heidegger, "Building, Dwelling, Thinking," in *Basic Writings: Revised and Expanded Edition*, ed. David Farrell Krell (New York: HarperCollins, 1993), 351 [GA 7, 151] (translation modified).

66. Foltz, *Inhabiting the Earth*, 161.

67. Heidegger, "Building, Dwelling, Thinking," 351 [GA 7, 151] (translation modified).

68. Heidegger, "Building, Dwelling, Thinking," 352 [GA 7, 152].

69. Heidegger, "Building, Dwelling, Thinking," 354 [GA 7, 154].

70. Heidegger, "The Question Concerning Technology," 16 [GA 7, 16].

71. Cf. Heidegger, "The Question Concerning Technology," 14 [GA 7, 14].

72. Heidegger, "The Question Concerning Technology," 14 [GA 7, 14].

73. Heidegger, *What Is Called Thinking?* 14 [GA 8, 26].

74. Heidegger, *What Is Called Thinking?* 23 [GA 8, 25].

75. Heidegger, *Being and Time*, 100 [GA 2, 95].

76. Remmon E. Barbaza, "There Where Nothing Happens," in *Heidegger and the Earth: Essays in Environmental Philosophy*, second edition, ed. Ladelle McWhorter and Gail Stenstad (Toronto, Buffalo, and London: University of Toronto Press, 2009), 193.

77. Martin Heidegger, "The Thing," 173 [GA 7, 174–175].

78. Heidegger, "The Thing," 174 [GA 7, 176].

79. Cf. Martin Heidegger, "Building, Dwelling, Thinking," 355 [GA 7, 155].

80. Heidegger, "The Thing," 179 [GA 7, 181].

81. Heidegger, "Building, Dwelling, Thinking," 349 [GA 7, 149].

82. Liddell and Scott, *An Intermediate Greek-English Lexicon*, 622.

83. Heidegger, "Building, Dwelling, Thinking," 356 [GA 7, 156].

84. Leopold, *A Sand County Almanac*, 9.

85. Heidegger, "The Thing," 181 [GA 7, 183].

86. Heidegger, *Discourse on Thinking*, 45 [GA 16, 518].

87. Heidegger, *Discourse on Thinking*, 47 [GA 16, 520].

88. Adam Sharr, *Heidegger's Hut* (Cambridge and London: The MIT Press, 2006), 1.

89. Martin Heidegger, "Why Do I Stay in the Provinces?" in *Heidegger: The Man and the Thinker*, ed. Thomas Sheehan (Chicago: Precedent, 1981), 28 [GA 13, 10–11].

90. Heidegger, "Why Do I Stay in the Provinces?" 27 [GA 13, 9–10].

91. Cf. Sharr, *Heidegger's Hut*, 46, 48, 53, 62.

92. Heidegger, "Building, Dwelling, Thinking," 363 [GA 7, 163].

93. Heidegger, "The Turning," 40 [GA 79, 71].

94. Heidegger, *What Is Called Thinking?* 31 [GA 8, 32].

95. Heidegger, *Discourse on Thinking*, 45 [GA 16, 518].

96. Heidegger, *Discourse on Thinking*, 45 [GA 16, 518].

97. An excellent Heideggerian analysis of this phenomenon can be found in Richard Polt, "A Heideggerian Critique of Cyberbeing," in *Horizons of Authenticity in Phenomenology, Existentialism, and Moral Psychology: Essays in Honor of Charles Guignon*, ed. Hans Pedersen and Megan Altman (Dordrecht, Heidelberg, New York, and London: Springer, 2015), chapter 12.

98. Heidegger, *Discourse on Thinking*, 53–54 [GA 16, 526].

99. Heidegger, *Discourse on Thinking*, 53 [GA 16, 526].

100. For the significance of Heidegger's term, *die Besinnung*, cf. Joan Stambaugh, "The Future of Continental Philosophy," in *Writing the Politics of Difference*, ed. Hugh J. Silverman (Albany: State University of New York Press, 1991), 278–279.

101. Heidegger, *Discourse on Thinking*, 55 [GA 16, 528].

102. Heidegger, *What Is Called Thinking?* 4 [GA 8, 6].

103. Heidegger, "The Turning," 39 [GA 79, 70] (translation modified).

104. Heidegger, *Pathmarks*, 260 [GA 9, 172].

105. Eric Sean Nelson, "Responding to Heaven and Earth: Daoism, Heidegger and Ecology," *Environmental Philosophy* 1, no. 2 (2004): 66.

Chapter Five

Cultivating a Non-Western Perspective

Through utilizing Heidegger's discussion of the history of being and his analysis of the contemporary period, we have tried to show how it came about that we have come to see all of nature as a giant inventory of resources to be maximally exploited. Heidegger shows the progression of Western metaphysics and how it has led to the contemporary period of enframing. His analysis of the Western metaphysical tradition has provided us with a way of understanding how our experience of reality has led to the environmental crisis. From this perspective, the emphasis on maximally exploiting nature, which has come to be seen solely in terms of human interests in the contemporary period, is the underlying reason behind the crisis. As Heidegger has argued, since this is a result of our metaphysical tradition, the only viable way out of the mode of enframing is to initiate a postmetaphysical understanding of being. Heidegger attempted to glimpse what this new understanding could look like through *Ereignis*. In the previous chapter, we looked at his notions of letting beings be, freedom, and dwelling to see what the human relation to nature could look like in the new beginning. In this chapter, I hope to show how Heidegger's vision of reality attempts to overcome Western metaphysics in that it resonates well with the thought one finds in philosophical Daoism, a non-Western tradition that Heidegger himself appreciated.

As mentioned in chapter 2, authors representing the deep ecology movement have turned to non-Western traditions such as Buddhism, Hinduism, and Daoism to try to come up with an environmental ethic that gets away from Western metaphysics. The problem with such accounts is that they do not recognize how entrenched concepts from the Western metaphysical tradition are in our understanding of reality. As Heidegger states, "Metaphysics cannot be abolished like an opinion,"[1] and, therefore, the deep-seated scaffolding that undermines our current metaphysical outlook must be brought to

87

light in order for us to make any significant shift in our ontological orientation. Heidegger gets us to see the metaphysical underpinnings of our environmental crisis and how they pervade our experience of the world, which is an
essential component in our quest to move beyond them. In this respect, he
thinks "more deeply" than deep ecologists who simply swap out destructive
Western concepts for "Eastern" ones. It is our task to move beyond Western
metaphysics and initiate a new understanding of human beings and their
relation to the natural world. Since Heidegger was heavily interested in
philosophical Daoism and found intellectual kinship with this tradition, we
will focus on Daoism in our quest to find an environmentally sustainable
ethic.[2] Peter Marshall has shown that Daoism is one of the earliest world
traditions to offer an ecological outlook. He states, "The first clear expression
of ecological thinking appears in ancient China from about the sixth century
BC. . . . The Daoists . . . offered the most profound and eloquent philosophy
of nature ever elaborated and the first stirrings of ecological sensibility."[3] I
will argue that aspects of Daoism not only show a deep resonance with Heidegger's later thinking, but also provide the sort of nonmetaphysical understanding of human beings and nature that Heidegger tried to cultivate in his
own thinking. In the end, our environmental ethic will turn out to be a
Heideggerian-*cum*-Daoist understanding of human beings and their place in
the natural world.

FROM HEIDEGGER TO DAOISM

Philosophical Daoism is a natural candidate for us to turn due to its affinity
with Heidegger's later philosophy. It has been well documented that Heidegger engaged with philosophical Daoism as early as 1930.[4] As his thought
matured, he became more and more enthralled with this ancient and foreign
way of thinking. In fact, in the summer of 1946, he attempted to translate the
greatest text from the Daoist tradition, Laozi's *Daodejing*, into German with
one of his Chinese students, Paul Shih-yi Hsiao, at his hut in Todtnauberg. In
recollecting his experience with Heidegger on this project, Hsiao notes that
he had the impression "that the work exerted a significant influence on Heidegger."[5] Scholars have debated as to how much influence Heidegger's dialogue with Daoism had on his own philosophy. At one end of the spectrum
are intellectuals who say that Laozi was "one of the decisive sources of the
later Heidegger"[6] or even go as far as saying that Heidegger may have
"intentionally incorporated East Asian ideas, in an encoded manner, into his
work."[7] At the other end are scholars like Chan-Fai Cheung who argue that
the relation between Heidegger and Daoism has been "over-interpreted and
exaggerated."[8] Regardless of how much his engagement with Daoist thought

influenced his own thinking, it is clear that Heidegger found an intellectual kinship with Daoism. Moreover, Gadamer has stated that Heidegger studies would benefit from the serious pursuit of comparisons of his work with Asian philosophies.[9] I will try to show how certain elements from the Daoist tradition resonate with the new beginning that Heidegger envisioned in his own later thought. Since Daoism is not a product of Western metaphysics and since it espouses an environmentally friendly perspective on the human place in nature, it may help in finding a sustainable vision of the human place in nature that goes beyond metaphysics.

The two most important works in the Daoist canon are the *Daodejing* [道德經] and the *Zhuangzi* [莊子]. Graham Parkes, an expert in both Heidegger and East Asian traditions, states that "a major impetus for Heidegger's 'new beginning' (as he himself calls it)—for the trajectory of a path of thinking that is to lead beyond (or around or beneath) Western metaphysics—came from non-Western sources."[10] He cites both Laozi [老子] and Zhuangzi [莊子] as essential sources for the later Heidegger.[11] Our question will not be how or to what extent Heidegger's new beginning was influenced by these texts but rather what he found in these ancient works that resonate with the aspects of his own thinking that are relevant to achieving a viable environmental ethic.[12]

While comparative philosophers have attempted to show the similarities between Heidegger's notion of being and the Daoist notion of *dào* or Heidegger's notion of the clearing and the Daoist notion of wú [無], the most obvious place to look for resonance between the two philosophies comes with Heidegger's notion of *Gelassenheit*, the idea that we should learn to let beings be the beings that they are and unfold on their own natural terms, and the Daoist notion of *wúwéi* [無為].[13] Commentators often point to Meister Eckhart as Heidegger's inspiration for his thoughts on letting beings be.[14] While Heidegger clearly utilized Eckhart as a primary source in his exposition of this concept, his idea of letting beings be also recalls the key Daoist term, *wúwéi*. As Joan Stambaugh notes, "The change from all subjectivistic reifying representational thinking to the kind of thinking or sensing Heidegger is trying to convey occurs through releasement (Gelassenheit). The Daoist equivalent for [Gelassenheit] is, of course, wúwéi."[15] Steven Burik has provided a persuasive argument that Heidegger's *Gelassenheit* and the Daoist notion of *wúwéi* are conceptually linked in that they are both beyond the distinction between activity and passivity, entail a deference to the natural unfolding of entities, and attempt to avoid artificial constructions.[16] It will be our task to validate the claims by Stambaugh and Burik and try to show how Heidegger's idea of letting beings be approaches the Daoist virtue of *wúwéi*. First we must get clear on what *wúwéi* means in its original context. Roger Ames and David Hall, two of the most respected Western commentators on philosophical Daoism, explain that *wúwéi* should be understood as "noncoercive actions in accordance with the dé of things."[17] In order to understand this, we must get clear on the crucial Daoist term *dé* [德], which only makes sense when juxtaposed with *dào* [道]. After doing so, we will be able to link up *wúwéi* with Heidegger's notion of letting beings be, i.e., *Gelassenheit*.

Dào is a notoriously obscure concept in Daoist literature. In the *Daodejing*, Laozi calls it "beyond form," "beyond sound," "intangible," and "indefinable."[18] The literal translation of *dào* is "way," but in the Daoist conception of nature, *dào* has a special significance. An apt description of the *dào* is the rhythmic way of nature that comes forth in a "relentless emergence of spontaneous novelty"[19] that nothing can escape since it "flows everywhere."[20] This emergence is spontaneous because there is no external mover that "pushes" things into presence. Rather than conceiving of nature as something that was produced (by the Christian God, for example), Laozi stresses that this process happens *zìrán* (自然), which literally means "self-so." With this concept, we can begin to see how Daoism can help us to get away from the productionistic tendencies we find in Western metaphysics. *Zìrán* is "the 'natural' or 'spontaneous' way things and events take by themselves."[21] If we are to show the relationship between the way of nature that is the *dào* and *zìrán*, we can say that the rhythmic way of nature should be understood as a process that happens "self-so." In flowing everywhere, the *dào* suffuses the entire world and allows things to develop along their own lines. Daoists stress that human beings should do their best to allow the *dào* to work without undue human interference.

In order to understand how the *dào* is immanent in the world, Laozi speaks of the *dé* of particular things. Like the *dào*, *dé* does not allow for a precise definition. It is variously translated into English as "efficacy," "power," and "virtue." Ames and Hall describe *dé* as a particular entity's way of "having [an] inherent virtue or power to produce effects."[22] In allowing things to be suffused by *dào*, i.e., in allowing beings to follow their own natural course, natural beings will exhibit their *dé*, which is their particular, unique way of flourishing. Laozi clearly understands *dào* and *dé* as complementary concepts. He states, "All things arise from *dào*. They are nourished by *dé*."[23] Every being is similar in that it is involved in the continuous process of change that is the *dào*, but every particular being is unique in that it has its own *dé*. In another chapter, Laozi states, "The greatest *dé* is to follow *dào* and *dào* alone."[24] What this means is that the best way to allow a being to flourish in its unique way is to simply allow it to follow the *dào*, which means allowing it to go its natural course. While there are similarities between the natural courses of beings of the same species, making their essential unfolding alike, Daoists stress that each particular being is unique. To understand any particular entity well, one must recognize its similarities with other beings of the same material makeup but also be attentive to its unique way of being.

The Daoist understanding of reality is very different than what we find in the central Western tradition. As we have seen, in Western metaphysics, the emphasis is placed on enduring presence.[25] To be a being is to be something that is stable and predictable, and thereby manipulable. Heidegger showed us how this emphasis on enduring presence leads to the contemporary epoch of enframing. Instead of stressing permanence and uniformity, the Daoists stress how each individual is constantly changing as it is in interplay with all other things, making entities *intrinsically connected*. Chang Chung-yuan explains the world that one finds in the Daoist framework as follows: "Each individual event in the world of events mutually and simultaneously enters, draws in, embraces, and is being embraced unimpededly. [Daoism] suggests the infinitely complicated interplay among all particularities in the world of events."[26] Instead of a world that is fixed and stable, the Daoist world is one in which each being is simultaneously affecting other beings in an unending, novel mutual interpenetration. Zhuangzi provides an analogy of the great pipes of nature that cover the entire universe and influence all things without causing interference to capture the world of Daoism: "The role of these forces on all forms of living things is not the same. . . . For each is different, using what they need to be, not influenced by any other force!"[27] Daoists understand the world as a rhythmic symphony of mutually interacting entities following *dào* without negatively affecting one another. This is the result of the workings between *dào* and *dé*.

WÚWÉI AND *GELASSENHEIT*

Now that we have a grasp as to what *dào* and *dé* mean, we can link up *wúwéi* with *dé*. Hall states, "*Wúwéi*, or nonassertive action, involves acting in accordance with the *dé* of things."[28] So when one practices *wúwéi*, one respects the natural way in which each entity unfolds. Since each particular entity has its own unique structure and its own way of flourishing in the world, the person who practices *wúwéi* must do one's best to allow this structure and way of flourishing to come forth and then respond to it accordingly. This requires not only knowledge of the workings of the ways of nature but also an openness to new ways in which entities come to presence, since there are always novel elements in one's experience with the natural world due to the unique particularity of any individual entity. Daoists speak of this in terms of a mirroring response. Hall explains, "*Wúwéi* involves a mirroring response. As such, it is action that, by taking the other on its own terms, defers to what it actually is. *Wúwéi* involves recognizing the continuity between oneself and the other, and responding in such a way that one's own actions promote the well-being both of oneself and the other."[29] As in *Gelassenheit*, the emphasis in mirroring is on deferring to the ways in which entities unfold on their own terms rather than applying a restrictive grid of knowledge onto things. In the *Zhuangzi*, this symbol of the mirror is prevalent. Here, Zhuangzi states, "The perfect man's heart is like a mirror. It does not search after things. It does not look for things. It does not seek knowledge, just responds."[30] The perfect man [*zhēnrén* / 真人] is Zhuangzi's name for the person who has achieved *wúwéi* in all of one's actions. In commenting on this passage, Katrin Froese states, "The *zhēnrén* mirrors the world in its immediacy, neither imposing a grid of knowledge on it, nor interpreting the present in terms of ideals of the future."[31] Instead of viewing things in accordance with a preset grid of expectations in accordance with one's interests (as, say, the Cartesian subject does or as scientists in the Western modern period do), one is to be attentively open to the various ways in which beings manifest themselves. In accomplishing this openness, one then acts in accordance with the natural way of things. Although a common translation of *wúwéi* is nonaction, it is clear that it is not a passive concept. Instead, *wúwéi* involves the sort of careful, considerate deference to the essential unfolding of entities as they are in themselves that Heidegger speaks of in his espousal of *Gelassenheit*.

Though Daoists speak of mirroring, it is not as though they believe that they can ever perfectly reflect reality as it is in its ever-emerging novelty. Since the ways in which things emerge into presence are always new, Daoists do not believe that they can ever get a completely perfect portrayal of the way reality is in and of itself. Indeed, Laozi's first line in the *Daodejing* is "The *dào* that can be told is not the eternal *dào*."[32] In other words, the rhythmic flow of nature resists any sort of exhaustive explanation. Therefore, as Froese states, "The act of mirroring does not imply that one uncover the unchanging essence that underlies things, but rather necessitates a sensitivity to its transitory particularity. [It] is an active search for the complementary relations between beings rather than a will to overpower them."[33] The aim in mirroring is to bring about the unique way in which an entity unfolds on its own terms without applying any sort of inappropriate interpretations on things that happen to match up with one's own expectations. In this way, it is a practice that is opposed to the tendencies of domination that we have seen in the Western metaphysical tradition and is in line with Heidegger's notion of letting beings be. Laozi's injunction is to "help everything find its own nature, but refrain from coercive action."[34]

One of the similarities that we can find between this Daoist practice and the sort of thinking that we found in the later Heidegger is the idea that practicing letting beings be or *Gelassenheit* involves the process of simultaneously letting things come into their own and allowing oneself to come into one's own. For Heidegger, when we let beings be, we are also coming into our own by becoming who we essentially are: the shepherds of being that are open to the ways in which entities come to presence, essentially unfold, and recede back into absence.[35] In the Daoist tradition, the emphasis is not explicitly on becoming shepherds of being but rather on recognizing the natural way in which things unfold and then following this natural way oneself. In the words of Arthur Danto, "If there is an injunction, it is to find the way the world wants to go and then to take that way oneself: and not to attempt to impose one's own order onto things, not to dominate."[36] One finds such injunctions throughout both the *Daodejing* and the *Zhuangzi*. However, since the book of *Zhuangzi* provides more vivid, concrete examples of this through looking at those who achieve *wúwéi* and thereby follow the natural course of things, we will look mainly at this text. These examples will allow us to get a sense as to what *wúwéi* entails, which will then allow us to show the clearest link between Heidegger's thought and Daoism.

The *Zhuangzi* is filled with tales of people who attain a mastery of their craft by practicing *wúwéi*. One such tale speaks of a swimmer who astonishes Confucius.[37] Zhuangzi states:

> Confucius was sightseeing in Lu Liang, where the waterfall is thirty fathoms high and the river races along for forty miles, so fast that neither fish nor any other creature can swim in it. He saw one person dive in and he assumed that this person wanted to embrace death, perhaps because of some anxiety, so he placed his followers along the bank and they prepared to pull him out. However, the swimmer, having gone a hundred yards, came out, and walked nonchalantly along the bank, singing a song with water dripping off of him.[38]

The swimmer is able to attain such an incredible feat because he follows the natural ways of the currents, rather than fighting against them. In a certain sense, the swimmer does not view himself as separate from the water, and is therefore able to follow its ebbs and flows. As the swimmer says, "I go with the currents and come out with the flow, just going with the *dào* of the water and never being concerned . . . I am not sure why I do this, but I am certain that this is my destiny."[39] In realizing one aspect of his nature, the swimmer in this passage follows the currents of the water and thereby is able to attain a mastery that astonishes others. One of the clear implications is that humans are able to accomplish incredible feats if they can simply learn to go with nature rather than oppose it.

Another famous example in the *Zhuangzi* of following the natural way of things comes from Cook Ding, a butcher who has not sharpened his blade in nineteen years, since he has attained such a mastery of the art of butchering oxen. When a prince asks how he has attained such mastery, he responds, "I see the natural lines and my knife slides through the great hollows, follows the great cavities, using that which is already there to my advantage." Upon hearing such a response, the prince states, "I have heard what Cook Ding has to say and from his words I have learned how to live life fully."[40] For Zhuangzi, what it means to live life fully is to follow the natural way of things in all activities. Whether this be a swimmer going with the flow of the tides or a butcher following the natural curvature of the oxen he carves, the best way to proceed is to use the natural configuration of things to bring about the best results, rather than fighting against them, which inevitably will lead to frustration. In deferring to the natural way in which things are, the characters spoken of in the *Zhuangzi* realize the most efficient means of proceeding in the world in respect to their particular activities.[41] Unlike in the contemporary period of enframing wherein efficiency is understood strictly in terms of human interests, this efficiency is understood in terms of what is naturally best. In the famous words of Laozi, "*Dào* abides in *wúwéi*, yet nothing is left undone."[42] By simply attuning oneself to the nature of things, one brings out the best results.

One must harness a respectful deference when practicing *wúwéi*. Zhuangzi believes that "all forms of life have their own distinct natures,"[43] and the perfect man is the person who is able to respect the particular natures of the things that he deals with and allow them to flourish in their own unique way. Zhuangzi states, "This was the way of the ancient one who followed the *dào*: . . . flexible and not fixed upon one idea, open-minded and without a guide."[44] Like Heidegger, Zhuangzi emphasizes that one should be open to the ways in which things unfold on their own terms, and this requires a deferential, rather than domineering attitude. Importantly, both Heidegger and Daoists stress the particularity of each individual entity and how one must be open to each being's essential unfolding. In his argument against scientism, Heidegger says, "a botanist, when he examines the labiate flower, will never be concerned about the single flower as a single one: it always remains an exemplar only."[45] Heidegger tries to restore a sense of uniqueness to entities in *Gelassenheit* by co-responding to the things themselves, in their own essential unfolding. In a similar way, the Daoist practice of *wúwéi* requires an attentive focus on each particular being in its unique context.

Heidegger's *Gelassenheit* and the Daoist practice of *wúwéi* are also similar in their espousal of the human relationship to technology. Heidegger explicitly says that "*Gelassenheit* towards technology is using technological devices but not allowing them to lay waste our nature."[46] In the *Zhuangzi*, we see a similar worry regarding the ability of technology to transform one's inner being or essence, which the Chinese refer to as *xīn* [心], a word commonly translated as "heart" or "mind." In coming across an older man working on his land by manually watering his crops, a younger man states, "There are machines which can water a hundred fields in one day, for very little effort but with much to show for it." Upon being asked why he does not use such machines, the older man responds, "where you have machines, then you get certain kinds of problems; where you get certain kinds of problems, then you find a *xīn* warped by these problems. Where you get a *xīn* warped, its purity and simplicity are disturbed. When purity and simplicity are disturbed, then the spirit is alarmed and an alarmed spirit is no place for the *dào* to dwell."[47] In Daoism, we do not find an outright rejection of technology, but there is a clear rejection of the type of technology that warps the human essence in that it allows for the presumption that humans are masters of the natural world. When activities come too easy with the use of technology, one loses an appreciation for things, which ultimately thwarts one's nature.

A NEW "ETHIC"

Now that we have shown the similarities between Heidegger's notion of letting beings be and the Daoist notion of *wúwéi* and how they can be used to understand and respond to enframing, we are finally in a position to indicate what a Heideggerian-*cum*-Daoist environmental ethic would entail. First, the "ethic" is not a type of normative ethics that has dominated environmental ethics in the past decades. Rather than a version of applied ethics, both Heidegger and Daoism espouse an ethics as *ethos*. Our word "ethos" is derived from the Greek word ἔθος [*ethos*], which means "custom" or "habit."[48] An ethic in this sense has more to do with practice than theory. Nelson explains what this means in the context of Daoism as follows:

> Although classical Daoist texts seem to reject "ethics," provided that ethics consists of rules, norms, and conventions organizing hierarchical and authority-driven social relations, early Daoism is not so much an anti-ethical and aesthetic nihilism as it is an *alternative way of living with things*. This naturalistic and anti-conventional approach to the ethical can be described preliminarily as an embodied receptivity to the myriad . . . things themselves in their specificity, parity, and interconnectedness.[49]

Heidegger's "new beginning" also evokes "an alternative way of living with things" in that the human being is to respect things *as* things and dwell among them accordingly. Since all things are perpetually changing, "interpretations of the same thing must stay in motion in order to remain loyal to the thing."[50] In Heidegger's *Contributions to Philosophy*, he states that he is striving to overcome the view that beings are to be understood as enduring presence and venture an attempt to grasp the "essential happening of the rank and uniqueness of beings in each instance."[51] This emphasis on respecting the particular things on their own terms is essential to a Heideggerian version of an environmental ethic, rather than a prescriptive or normative theory. Moreover, this ontological orientation is linked with ethics, as David Webb explains: "Since ontological thought remains planted in our concrete experience, it is bound to the existential concern over who we are and how we live; that is, ontology is inseparable from ethics."[52]

The Daoist view of the world is similar to Heidegger's in that Daoists refuse to posit essential, stable, permanent substances. From the Daoist point of view, the world is a continually novel stream of entities that come to presence, flourish, decay, and recede again into absence. Zhuangzi states, "In the growth of all life, their roots and buds have their appointed place and distinct shape, and from this comes maturation and then decay, the constant stream of transformation and change."[53] The natural world is one of constant flux and ever-emerging novelty, meaning that one can never get a firm handle on it. As Ames and Hall state, "The Daoist does not posit the existence of some permanent reality behind appearances, some unchanging substratum, some essential defining aspect behind the accidents of change."[54] Rather, in the Daoist worldview, "particular 'things' are in fact processual events, and are thus *intrinsically* related to other 'things' that provide them context."[55]

One can begin to see the connection between having a relational worldview and having knowledge of the interdependence of things. In Daoism, one cannot separate a being from its environment, since its health and flourishing depends on it. In this sense, the Daoist worldview is more in tune with the scientific understanding of the way in which individuals within ecosystems work, since they can better account for the interdependence of entities. Martin Schönfeld shows how this ontological orientation leads to a proper response to the climate crisis. He states:

> Climate change shows, in ontological terms, that the biosphere is one comprehensive energetic system, a network of happenings, whose structure is informed by pervasive pulses, and in which everyone, without exception, is tied to the dynamics of the [earth] . . . Daoists can actually congratulate themselves on engaging with an ontological perspective that is more commensurate with our science than any rivaling metaphysical image.[56]

Schönfeld makes an important point here. The fact that Daoists view all entities as interconnected entails that human practices not only affect their immediate environments but even affect the climate of the earth as such. As we have seen in chapter 1 with our discussion of how anthropogenic climate change is changing the dynamics of the earth that we have come to know and take for granted, the practices we engage in affect the health of the planet as such, which ultimately affects us. Daoism can get us to recognize the interdependence of all things and provide us with a new perspective of the ways in which human actions affect nature.

In line with this Daoist insight comes Heidegger's idea that all entities in any given system are interdependent. The commitment to holism, or the idea that things only make sense when viewed as a whole, is a strand that runs throughout Heidegger's thought. In *Being and Time*, Heidegger states, "there 'is' no such thing as *an* equipment. To the Being of any equipment there always belongs a totality of equipment, in which it can be the equipment that it is."[57] He goes on to show how one cannot make sense of a pen that one is using, for instance, unless one takes into consideration its relation with all other elements in the room. In order for a pen to function *as* a pen, it requires ink, an ink-stand, paper to write on, a desk, and so forth. Heidegger claims that one cannot understand a pen as a piece of equipment without taking its surroundings into consideration. The idea of interdependence that comes with this commitment to holism comes out clearly in his later work, "The Thing." Here, as discussed in chapter 4, Heidegger speaks of the essence of the outpouring of a jug of wine to be interconnected with the earth, sky, divinities, and mortals. This simple act depends on the health of the soil to grow the grapes, and is thereby dependent on earth, the good weather from the sky, the cultivation of the grapes by human beings, and even the divinities in certain contexts.[58] David Goicoechea has argued that Heidegger's understanding of the fourfold was deliberately taken from Laozi's philosophy.[59] Regardless of whether Laozi is a true influence, Heidegger tries to get us to think of how each of these elements are interconnected with the notion of the fourfold [*das Geviert*] in his later thought, which offers an understanding of things that is interrelational and interdependent. In this way, Heidegger approaches a worldview that is in tune with our understanding that each being depends on others, which also implies that one's own actions affect other beings in the long run even if this is not immediately clear.

The question remains as to what a Heideggerian-*cum*-Daoist environmental ethic might look like. Clearly, *Gelassenheit* and *wúwéi* are the ideal practices of such an ethic, along with an emphasis on the interrelatedness and interdependence of natural things. On an individualistic scale, I have argued that Heidegger's own life during his days at his hut may be a fitting example of what this may look like in practice. One possible image of this way of dwelling on the earth on a communal scale may be found in the Daoist hermitages that have existed in remote Chinese landscapes for centuries. John Blofield, a British writer who traveled to one such hermitage in the 1930s, provides a picture of what such dwelling can entail, which I quote at length:

> The recluses' love of unspoiled beauty had not deterred them from lending nature a helping hand. The immediate environs of the Valley Spirit Hermitage

gave the impression of a series of rocks and caverns, overhung by ferns and luxuriant plants, which just happened to emerge from the undergrowth in this vicinity, adding enormously to its picturesqueness. . . . There was, of course, no obvious symmetry, but yet a sense of underlying harmony that was just a shade too pronounced to be altogether natural. Whoever had been responsible for making the "guided wildness" of the approach to the hermitage even lovelier than nature's untouched handiwork had surely been a master of subtlety, for there was not an object within sight of the stairway of which one could confidently affirm it had been tampered with. . . . In landscaping, the underlying principle was to avoid artificiality not by refraining from improving on natural forms, but by bringing out or highlighting shapes—beautiful, amusing or grotesque—already inherent in the objects worked upon. A square should not be rounded, but a rough sphere could be made rounder; a shrub should be made to resemble a stork only if the stork already existed potentially in the plant's natural shape; water might be diverted from one pile of rocks to another to heighten the beauty of a cataract, but only if there were nothing inherently unnatural in the resulting flow and fall. Nature could be assisted to achieve masterly effects, but the concept in the improver's mind must in itself be based on intimate knowledge of nature's manifestations. In short, the aim in most cases was to assist nature to do what it might under more favorable circumstances have done for itself.[60]

While replicating this version of a communal commitment to *wúwéi* is not a live option for many human beings living in the contemporary period, one can regard it as an ideal for which to strive. Importantly, embracing such an existence does not entail a passive indifference to things, nor does it presume that humans can master over the natural world as they see fit. Rather, a middle ground is found wherein things are respected on their own terms and yet taken care of by human beings, who are uniquely positioned to preserve natural beings as they are in themselves and yet aid them in their flourishing. A *respons*iveness to things as they are in themselves prompts a *respons*ibility to allow them to unfold in their own unique ways, which brings out the best version of things when given a helping hand.

In order to cultivate such a responsiveness and responsibility, one must interact with the natural world in ways that are foreign to many people living in the age of modern technology, who have come to attain their food from the supermarket, get their water from the faucet, and think of "nature" as the space between cities. In becoming so detached from the natural world, one cannot respect or care for nature. A Heideggerian-*cum*-Daoist environmental ethic would entail living closer to nature by respecting natural things *as* things of the relational totality that is the natural world. The great environmental philosopher John Muir provides a fitting pronouncement to guide a closer bond with nature: "Let children walk with Nature, let them see the beautiful blendings and communions of death and life, their joyous inseparable unity, as taught in woods and meadows, plains and mountains and streams."[61] When such an intimate understanding of nature is cultivated, one can begin to respect the natural as more beautiful and worthy of respect than anything artificially constructed to fulfill human interests. On his famous thousand-mile walk from Indiana to the Gulf of Mexico in 1867, Muir came across a starkly contrasting scene near the Mammoth Caves in Kentucky, which he describes as follows: "I never before saw Nature's grandeur in so abrupt contrast with paltry artificial gardens. The fashionable hotel grounds are in exact parlor taste, with many a beautiful plant cultivated to deformity, and arranged in strict geometrical beds, the whole pretty affair a laborious failure side by side with Divine beauty."[62] If we can cultivate an appreciation for the natural world on its own terms and respond in accordance with its essential unfolding, we will inevitably develop a sense of responsibility to maintain nature. As Nelson rightly explains, "The ethical is immanently lived and enacted in the *ethos* of its dwelling, i.e., in Dasein's art and manner of existing, rather than operating according to an external logic of function, norm, reason, [or] virtue."[63] If we situate the ethical as *ethos* with an eye towards nature, one's everyday practical existence becomes linked with ethical concerns for the natural world. Such a shift in one's ontological orientation and being-in-the-world is a still a possibility, as Heidegger reminds us:

> We are thinking of the possibility that the world civilization that is just now beginning might one day overcome its technological-scientific-industrial character not as the sole criterion of man's world sojourn. This may happen, not of and through itself, but in virtue of the readiness of man for a determination which, whether heeded or not, always speaks of the destiny of man, which has not yet been decided.[64]

The destiny of the human race has yet to be determined.

CONCLUSION

Parkes has argued convincingly that "Daoism is one of those practice-based philosophies of self-transformation in which new understanding goes hand in hand with a change not only in attitude but also in behavior."[65] In this regard, Parkes sees harmony with Heidegger's later thought.[66] I have tried to argue that a basic understanding of the Daoist practice of *wúwéi* gives us a sense as to what living in accordance with *Gelassenheit* might look like from an environmental perspective. If one learns to live in accordance with *Gelassenheit*, one has properly attained dwelling. Heidegger's days at his hut in Todtnauberg are an example of what this might look like on an individual scale, while the communal living of Daoists at the Valley Spirit Hermitage might provide us with an example on a wider scale. Such examples elicit a deep connection between one's thinking and living, which is a connection that is sometimes lost in contemporary versions of ethics, especially when dealing with normative versions of "applied ethics." From a Heideggerian-*cum*-Daoist perspective, there is no fundamental disconnect between thinking and living. Given the immensity of the environmental crisis, we face the ultimate decision of the fate of human beings. Are we capable of opening our perspectives to new and more appropriate ways of understanding the human relationship to the natural world or will we continue to master the natural world through our technological and scientific progress? A fitting answer to this question comes from Heidegger's favorite poet, Friedrich Hölderlin, who says:

> But where danger is, grows
> *The saving power also.*[67]

NOTES

1. Heidegger, "Overcoming Metaphysics," 85 [GA 7, 69].

2. By focusing on Daoism, I do not wish to imply that other traditions are not helpful in our quest to build a viable environmental ethic. Many non-Western traditions could be used in such an effort. I focus on Daoism because it resonates most with Heidegger's thought.

3. Peter Marshall, *Nature's Web: Rethinking Our Place on Earth* (New York: Paragon House, 1993), 9. "Taoism," "Taoists," or "tao" are all equivalent to "Daoism," "Daoists," or "dao." Many earlier Western commentators and translators on Chinese thought adopted the Wade-Giles system, but most people now adopt Pinyin. I will utilize Pinyin for the sake of consistency.

4. Cf. Reinhard May, *Heidegger's Hidden Sources: East Asian Influences on His Work*, trans. Graham Parkes (New York: Routledge, 1996), 3.

5. Paul Shih-yi Hsiao, "Heidegger and Our Translation of the *Tao Te Ching*," in *Heidegger and Asian Thought*, ed. Graham Parkes (Honolulu: University of Hawaii Press, 1987), 93.

6. Guenter Wohlfart, "Heidegger and Laozi: *Wu* (Nothing)—On Chapter 11 of the *Daodejing*," *Journal of Chinese Philosophy* 30, no. 1 (2003): 52.

7. May, *Heidegger's Hidden Sources*, 9.

8. This quote comes from Lin Ma, *Heidegger on East-West Dialogue: Anticipating the Event* (New York and London: Routledge, 2008), 16. The original source is from Chan-Fai Cheung, "One World or Many Worlds? On Intercultural Understanding," in *Phenomenology of Interculturality and Life-World*, ed. Ernst W. Orth and Chan-Fai Cheung (Frieburg/Munchen: Verlag Karl Alber, 1998), 156.

9. Graham Parkes, "Introduction," in *Heidegger and Asian Thought*, ed. Graham Parkes (Honolulu: University of Hawaii Press, 1987), 5.

10. Graham Parkes, "Preface," in *Heidegger's Hidden Sources: East Asian Influences on His Work*, by Reinhard May (New York: Routledge, 1996), x.

11. Parkes, "Preface," xi.

12. For answers to the first question, the reader should consult May's *Heidegger's Hidden Sources* and Lin Ma, *Heidegger on East-West Dialogue: Anticipating the Event* (New York and London: Routledge, 2008).

13. For the link between *Sein* and *dào*, cf. Kwang-sae Lee, *East and West: Fusion of Horizons* (Paramus, N.J.: Homa & Sekey, 2006), 75. For the link between *Lichtung* and *wú*, cf. David Chai, "Nothingness and the Clearing: Heidegger, Daoism and the Quest for Primal Clarity," *The Review of Metaphysics* 67, no. 3 (2014): 583–601.

14. Cf. John Caputo, *The Mystical Element in Heidegger's Thought* (New York: Fordham University Press, 1986), xviii; Otto Pöggeler, *The Paths of Heidegger's Life and Thought*, trans. John Bailiff (Amherst, N.Y.: Prometheus, 1999), 292; and Bret W. Davis, *Heidegger and the Will: On the Way to* Gelassenheit (Evanston, Ill.: Northwestern University Press, 2007), chapter 5.

15. Joan Stambaugh, "Heidegger, Taoism, and the Question of Metaphysics," in *Heidegger and Asian Thought*, ed. Graham Parkes (Honolulu: University of Hawaii Press, 1987), 85. Note here that Stambaugh translates *Gelassenheit* as releasement, which is a common translation, since the aim is to get away from objectifying tendencies. I have chosen to translate it as letting beings be to stress the *lassen* (letting) aspect.

16. Cf. Steven Burik, *The End of Comparative Philosophy and the Task of Comparative Thinking: Heidegger, Derrida, and Daoism* (Albany: State University of New York Press, 2009), 159–160.

17. Roger T. Ames and David L. Hall, "Philosophical Introduction: Correlative Cosmology—An Interpretive Context" in *Daodejing: "Making This Life Significant": A Philosophical Translation* (New York: Ballantine, 2003), 38.

18. Lao Tsu, *Tao Te Ching*, trans. Gia-Fu Feng and Jane English (New York: Vintage Books, 1972), 14. The number refers to the chapter rather than the page.

19. Roger T. Ames, "The Local and the Focal in Realizing a Daoist World," in *Daoism and Ecology: Ways within a Cosmic Landscape*, ed. N. J. Girardot, James Miller, and Liu Xiaogan (Cambridge, Mass.: Harvard University Press, 2001), 267.

20. Lao Tsu, *Tao Te Ching*, 34.

21. Hans-Georg Moeller, *Daoism Explained: From the Dream of the Butterfly to the Fishnet Allegory* (Chicago and La Salle, Ill.: Open Court, 2004), 35.

22. Ames and Hall, "Philosophical Introduction," 61.

23. Lao Tsu, *Tao Te Ching*, 51.

24. Lao Tsu, *Tao Te Ching*, 21.

25. There are, of course, exceptions to this general statement. Heraclitus's philosophy shows many similarities to what can be found in Daoism. Other Western "process philosophies" espoused by thinkers like Spinoza and Whitehead share similarities as well.

26. Chang Chung-yuan, *Creativity and Taoism: A Study of Chinese Philosophy, Art, and Poetry* (New York: Harper & Row, 1963), 70.

27. Chuang Tzu, *The Book of Chuang Tzu*, trans. Martin Palmer (New York: Penguin, 2006), 9.

28. David L. Hall, "From Reference to Deference: Daoism and the Natural World," in *Daoism and Ecology: Ways Within a Cosmic Landscape*, ed. N. J. Girardot, James Miller, and Liu Xiaogan (Cambridge, Mass.: Harvard University Press, 2001), 256.

29. Hall, "From Reference to Deference," 257.

30. Chuang Tzu, *The Book of Chuang Tzu*, 64.

31. Katrin Froese, *Nietzsche, Heidegger, and Daoist Thought: Crossing Paths In-Between* (Albany: State University of New York Press, 2006), 108.

32. Lao Tzu, *Tao Te Ching*, 1.

33. Froese, *Nietzsche, Heidegger, and Daoist Thought*, 108.

34. Lao Tzu, *Tao Te Ching*, 64 (translation modified).

35. Heidegger says "the essential swaying is not limited to 'presence' " in the new beginning. Cf. *Contributions to Philosophy*, 52–53 [GA 65, 74–77]. David Chai argues that this understanding "was without question influenced by Eastern philosophy, specifically that of Daoism" in "Nothingness and the Clearing," 583.

36. Arthur C. Danto, *Mysticism and Morality: Oriental Thought and Moral Philosophy* (New York: Columbia University Press, 1987), 110–111.

37. In many passages of the *Zhuangzi*, Zhuangzi uses the character of Confucius [Kongzi] as a foil for his own sort of thinking. Confucians are mocked for being too superficial and not truly attaining the *dào*, since their moral system forces humans to act in a certain way, which Zhuangzi thinks is disingenuous.

38. Chuang Tzu, *The Book of Chuang Tzu*, 161–162.

39. Chuang Tzu, *The Book of Chuang Tzu*, 162.

40. Chuang Tzu, *The Book of Chuang Tzu*, 23.

41. There are many other examples of *wúwéi* in the *Zhuangzi*, including a wheelwright (chapter 13) and a woodcarver (chapter 19). The emphasis in any activity that cultivates *wúwéi* is on understanding the natural ways of things and acting in accordance with them. Modern-day examples include sailing wherein one must know the winds to be successful and skiing wherein one must go with the flow of the slopes.

42. Lao Tzu, *Tao Te Ching*, 37.

43. Chuang Tzu, *The Book of Chuang Tzu*, 189.

44. Chuang Tzu, *The Book of Chuang Tzu*, 301.

45. Heidegger, *What Is a Thing?* 15 [GA 41, 14].

46. Heidegger, *Discourse on Thinking*, 54 [GA 16, 526].

47. Chuang Tzu, *The Book of Chuang Tzu*, 99.

48. Liddell and Scott, *An Intermediate Greek-English Lexicon*, 226.

49. Eric Sean Nelson, "Responding with Dao: Early Daoist Ethics and the Environment," *Philosophy East and West* 59, no. 3 (2009): 294.

50. Polt, *The Emergency of Being*, 12.

51. Heidegger, *Contributions to Philosophy*, 46 [GA 65, 66] (translation modified).

52. David Webb, *Heidegger, Ethics, and the Practice of Ontology* (London and New York: Continuum, 2009), 5.

53. Chuang Tzu, *The Book of Chuang Tzu*, 110.

54. Ames and Hall, "Philosophical Translation," 14.

55. Ames and Hall, "Philosophical Translation," 15.

56. Martin Schönfeld, "How 'Real' Is Daoism? Triangulating Laozi, Kant, and Climate," *International Journal for Field-Being* 6, no. 1 (2007): 8–9.

57. Heidegger, *Being and Time*, 97 [GA 2, 92].

58. Cf. Heidegger, "The Thing," 178–179 [GA 7, 179–180] especially. We should point out that Laozi speaks in a similar way about a clay vessel in chapter 11 of the *Daodejing*. May argues that Heidegger appropriates this idea directly from Laozi in *Heidegger's Hidden Sources*, 30–31. Regardless of whether this is the case, it is clear that the idea of an interconnectivity is a common thread for both thinkers.

59. David Goicoechea, "Heidegger—The Taoists—Kierkegaard," *Journal of Chinese Philosophy* 30, no. 1 (2003): 90.

60. John Blofield, *The Secret and the Sublime: Daoist Mysteries and Magic* (New York: Dutton, 1973), 116–118.

61. John Muir, *A Thousand-Mile Walk to the Gulf*, ed. William Frederic Bade (Boston and New York: Houghton Mifflin, 1916), 70–71.

62. Muir, *A Thousand-Mile Walk to the Gulf*, 11–12.

63. Eric Sean Nelson, "Heidegger and the Questionability of the Ethical," *Studia Phaenomenologica* 8, no. 1 (2008): 422.

64. Heidegger, "The End of Philosophy and the Task of Thinking," 437 [GA 14, 75].

65. Graham Parkes, "Lao-Zhuang and Heidegger on Nature and Technology," *Journal of Chinese Philosophy* 39, no. 4 (2012): 114.

66. Parkes, "Lao-Zhuang and Heidegger on Nature and Technology," 114.

67. Cf. Heidegger, "The Question Concerning Technology," 34 [GA 7, 35].

Bibliography

Ames, Roger T. "The Local and the Focal in Realizing a Daoist World." In *Daoism and Ecology: Ways within a Cosmic Landscape*, edited by N. J. Girardot, James Miller, and Liu Xiaogan, 265–282. Cambridge, Mass.: Harvard University Press, 2001.

Ames, Roger T. and David L. Hall. "Philosophical Introduction: Correlative Cosmology—An Interpretive Context." In *Daodejing: "Making This Life Significant": A Philosophical Translation*, edited by Roger T. Ames and David L. Hall, 11–54. New York: Ballantine, 2003.

Augustine, Saint. *Concerning The City of God against the Pagans*. Translated by Henry Bettenson. London and New York: Penguin, 1984.

Bacon, Francis. *Meditations Sacræ*. In *Meditations Sacræ and Human Philosophy*, 67–71. Whitefish, Mont.: Kessinger Publishing, 1996.

———. *New Organon*. Edited by Lisa Jardine and Michael Silverthorne. Cambridge: Cambridge University Press, 2000.

———. *The Philosophy of Francis Bacon*. Translated by Benjamin Farrington. Chicago: University of Chicago Press, 1964.

Bannon, Bryan. *From Mastery to Mystery: A Phenomenological Foundation for an Environmental Ethic*. Athens: Ohio University Press, 2014.

Barbaza, Remmon E. "There Where Nothing Happens." In *Heidegger and the Earth: Essays in Environmental Philosophy*, second edition, edited by Ladelle McWhorter and Gail Stenstad, 186–200. Toronto, Buffalo, and London: University of Toronto Press, 2009.

Barnosky, Anthony D. et al. "Has the Earth's Sixth Mass Extinction Already Arrived?" *Nature* 471, no. 7336 (2011): 51–57.

Blofield, John. *The Secret and the Sublime: Daoist Mysteries and Magic*. New York: Dutton, 1973.

Braver, Lee. *Heidegger's Later Writings: A Reader's Guide*. London and New York: Continuum, 2009.

Broome, John. *Climate Matters: Ethics in a Warming World*. New York: W.W. Norton, 2012.

Brown, Charles S. and Ted Toadvine. "Eco-Phenomenology: An Introduction." In *Eco-Phenomenology: Back to the Earth Itself*, edited by Charles S. Brown and Ted Toadvine, ix–xxi. Albany: State University of New York Press, 2003.

Brown, Lester. *World on the Edge: How to Prevent Environmental and Economic Collapse*. New York and London: W. W. Norton & Company, 2011.

Burik, Steven. *The End of Comparative Philosophy and the Task of Comparative Thinking: Heidegger, Derrida, and Daoism*. Albany: State University of New York Press, 2009.

Butterfield, Herbert. *The Origins of Modern Science: 1300–1800*. London: G. Bell and Sons, 1958.

———. *The Cambridge History of Later Medieval Philosophy: From the Rediscovery of Aristotle to the Disintegration of Scholasticism: 1100–1600*. Edited by Norman Kretzmann, Anthony Kenny, and Jan Pinborg. Cambridge: Cambridge University Press, 1982.

Caputo, John. *The Mystical Element in Heidegger's Thought*. New York: Fordham University Press, 1986.

Carson, Rachel. *Silent Spring*. Boston: Houghton Mifflin, 1962.

Chai, David. "Nothingness and the Clearing: Heidegger, Daoism and the Quest for Primal Clarity." *The Review of Metaphysics* 67, no. 3 (2014): 583–601.

Cheung, Chan-Fai. "One World or Many Worlds? On Intercultural Understanding." In *Phenomenology of Interculturality and Life-World*, edited by Ernst W. Orth and Chan-Fai Cheung, 150–171. Frieburg/Munchen: Verlag Karl Alber, 1998.

Chuang Tzu. *The Book of Chuang Tzu*. Translated by Martin Palmer. New York: Penguin, 2006.

Chung-yuan, Chang. *Creativity and Taoism: A Study of Chinese Philosophy, Art, and Poetry*. New York: Harper & Row, 1963.

———. *Climate Change Geoengineering: Philosophical Perspectives, Legal Issues, and Governance Frameworks*. Edited by William C. G. Burns and Andrew L. Strauss. Cambridge: Cambridge University Press, 2013.

Crutzen, Paul J. "Albedo Enhancement by Stratospheric Sulfur Injections: A Contribution to Resolve a Policy Dilemma?" *Climatic Change* 77, no. 3–4 (2006): 211–220.

———. "Geology of Mankind." *Nature* 415, no. 6867 (2002): 23.

Dampier, William. *A Shorter History of Science*. New York: Meridian Books, 1957.

Danto, Arthur C. *Mysticism and Morality: Oriental Thought and Moral Philosophy*. New York: Columbia University Press, 1987.

Davion, Victoria. "Ecofeminism." In *A Companion to Environmental Philosophy*, edited by Dale Jamieson, 233–248. Malden, Mass.: Blackwell, 2001.

Davis, Bret W. *Heidegger and the Will: On the Way to* Gelassenheit. Evanston, Ill.: Northwestern University Press, 2007.

Deluca, Kevin Michael. "Thinking with Heidegger: Rethinking Environmental Theory and Practice." *Ethics and the Environment* 10, no. 1 (2005): 67–87.

Descartes, René. *Discourse on Method*. In *René Descartes: Philosophical Essays and Correspondence*, edited by Roger Ariew, 46–82. Indianapolis: Hackett Publishing Company, 2000.

———. *Principles of Philosophy*. In *René Descartes: Philosophical Essays and Correspondence*, edited by Roger Ariew, 222–272. Indianapolis: Hackett Publishing Company, 2000.

————. *Rules for the Direction of the Mind*. In *René Descartes: Philosophical Essays and Correspondence*, edited by Roger Ariew, 2–27. Indianapolis: Hackett Publishing Company, 2000.

————. "To Hyperaspistes, August 1641." In *The Philosophical Writings of Descartes, Volume III: The Correspondence*, translated by John Cottingham et al., 188–196. Cambridge: Cambridge University Press, 1991.

————. "To the Marquis of Newcastle." In *René Descartes: Philosophical Essays and Correspondence*, edited by Roger Ariew, 275–276. Indianapolis: Hackett Publishing Company, 2000.

————. "To Mersenne, On J.-B. Morin's Proof for the Existence of God (January 28, 1641)." In *René Descartes: Philosophical Essays and Correspondence*, edited by Roger Ariew, 95–96. Indianapolis and Cambridge: Hackett Publishing Company, 2000.

Devall, Bill and George Sessions. *Deep Ecology: Living As If Nature Mattered*. Layton, Utah: Gibbs M. Smith Inc., 1985.

Dreyfus, Hubert L. *Being-in-the-World: A Commentary on Heidegger's* Being and Time*, Division I*. Cambridge and London: The MIT Press, 1991.

————. "Heidegger on the Connection between Nihilism, Art, Technology, and Politics." In *The Cambridge Companion to Heidegger*, edited by Charles Guignon, 289–316. Cambridge: Cambridge University Press, 1993.

Elden, Stuart. "Contributions to Geography? The Spaces of Heidegger's *Beiträge*." *Environment and Planning D: Society and Space* 23, no. 6 (2005): 811–827.

Evernden, Neil. *The Natural Alien: Humankind and Environment*, second edition. Toronto: University of Toronto Press, 1999.

Faye, Emmanuel. *Heidegger: The Introduction of Nazism into Philosophy*. New Haven, Conn.: Yale University Press, 2009.

Foltz, Bruce. *Inhabiting the Earth: Heidegger, Environmental Ethics, and the Metaphysics of Nature*. Amherst, N.Y.: Humanity Books, 1995.

Fried, Gregory. *Heidegger's Polemos: From Being to Politics*. New Haven, Conn. and London: Yale University Press, 2000.

————. "Heidegger, Politics, and Us: Towards a Polemical Ethics." *Philosophy and Social Criticism* 39, no. 9 (2013): 863–875.

Froese, Katrin. *Nietzsche, Heidegger, and Daoist Thought: Crossing Paths In-Between*. Albany: State University of New York Press, 2006.

Gadamer, Hans-Georg. "Heidegger's Later Philosophy." In *Philosophical Hermeneutics*, translated by David E. Linge, 213–228. Berkeley: University of California Press, 1976.

Goicoechea, David. "Heidegger—The Taoists—Kierkegaard." *Journal of Chinese Philosophy* 30, no. 1 (2003): 81–97.

Guignon, Charles. *Heidegger and the Problem of Knowledge*. Indianapolis: Hackett Publishing Company, 1983.

————. "Heidegger's Concept of Freedom, 1927-1930." In *Interpreting Heidegger: Critical Essays*, edited by Daniel O. Dahlstrom, 79–105. Cambridge: Cambridge University Press, 2011.

————. "The History of Being." In *A Companion to Heidegger*, edited by Hubert Dreyfus and Mark Wrathall, 392–406. Malden, Mass.: Blackwell, 2005.

————. "Introduction." In *The Cambridge Companion to Heidegger*, edited by Charles Guignon, 1–41. Cambridge: Cambridge University Press, 1993.

————. "Martin Heidegger: *Being and Time*." In *Central Works of Philosophy Volume 4: The Twentieth Century: Moore to Popper*, edited by John Shand, 92–110. Montreal and Kingston: McGill-Queen's University Press, 2006.

Habermas, Jürgen. Mit Heidegger gegen Heidegger denken. Zur Veröffenlichung von Vorlesungen aus dem Jahre 1935. *Frankfurter Allgemeine Zeitung* (Frankfurt, Germany), July 25, 1953.

————. "Work and *Weltanschauung*: The Heidegger Controversy from a German Perspective." In *Heidegger: A Critical Reader*, edited by Hubert L. Dreyfus and Harrison Hall, 186–208. Cambridge, Mass.: Blackwell, 1992.

Hall, David L. "From Reference to Deference: Daoism and the Natural World." In *Daoism and Ecology: Ways Within a Cosmic Landscape*, edited by N. J. Girardot, James Miller, and Liu Xiaogan, 245–264. Cambridge, Mass.: Harvard University Press, 2001.

Hallam, A. and P. B. Wignall. *Mass Extinctions and Their Aftermath*. Oxford: Oxford University Press, 1997.

Hansen, James. "The Threat to the Planet." *New York Review of Books* 53, no. 12 (2006): 12–16.

Hardin, Garrett. "The Tragedy of the Commons." *Science* 162, no. 3859 (1968): 1243–1248.

Haszeldine, R. Stuart. "Carbon Capture and Storage: How Green Can Black Be?" *Science* 325, no. 5948 (2009): 1647–1652.

Heidegger, Martin. "The Age of the World Picture." In *The Question Concerning Technology and Other Essays*, translated by William Lovitt, 115–154. New York: Harper & Row, 1977.

————. "The Anaximander Fragment." In *Early Greek Thinking: The Dawn of Western Philosophy*, translated by David Farrell Krell and Frank A. Capuzzi, 13–58. San Francisco: Harper & Row, 1975.

————. *Basic Concepts of Aristotelian Philosophy*. Translated by Robert D. Metcalf and Mark B. Tanzer. Bloomington and Indianapolis: Indiana University Press, 2009.

————. *The Basic Problems of Phenomenology*, revised edition. Translated by Albert Hofstadter. Bloomington and Indianapolis: Indiana University Press, 1982.

————. *Being and Time*. Translated by John Macquarrie and Edward Robinson. New York: Harper & Row, 1962.

————. "Building, Dwelling, Thinking." In *Basic Writings: Revised and Expanded Edition*, edited by David Farrell Krell, 343–363. New York: HarperCollins, 1993.

————. *Contributions to Philosophy (From Enowning)*. Translated by Parvis Emad and Kenneth Maly. Bloomington and Indianapolis: Indiana University Press, 1999.

————. *Country Path Conversations*. Translated by Bret W. Davis. Bloomington and Indianapolis: Indiana University Press, 2010.

————. *Discourse on Thinking*. Translated by John M. Anderson and E. Hans Freund. New York, Hagerstown, San Francisco, London: Harper & Row, 1966.

————. "The End of Philosophy and the Task of Thinking." In *Basic Writings*, revised and expanded edition, edited by David Farrell Krell, 427–449. New York: HarperCollins, 1993.

———. *The Essence of Human Freedom: An Introduction to Philosophy*. Translated by Ted Sadler. New York and London: Continuum, 2002.

———. *Four Seminars*. Translated by Andrew Mitchell and François Raffoul. Bloomington and Indianapolis: Indiana University Press, 2003.

———. *Fundamental Concepts of Metaphysics: World, Finitude, Solitude*. Edited by William McNeil and Nicholas Walker. Bloomington: Indiana University Press, 1995.

———. *Identity and Difference*. Translated by Joan Stambaugh. Chicago and London: The University of Chicago Press, 2002.

———. *Introduction to Metaphysics*, second edition. Translated by Gregory Fried and Richard Polt. New Haven and London: Yale University Press, 2014.

———. "Logos (Heraclitus, Fragment B 50)." In *Early Greek Thinking: The Dawn of Western Philosophy*, translated by David Farrell Krell and Frank A. Capuzzi, 59–78. San Francisco: Harper & Row, 1975.

———. "Metaphysics as History of Being." In *The End of Philosophy*, translated by Joan Stambaugh, 1–54. Chicago: The University of Chicago Press, 1973.

———. *Mindfulness*. Translated by Parvis Emad and Thomas Kalary. New York and London: Continuum, 2006.

———. *Nietzsche, Volume III: The Will to Power as Knowledge and as Metaphysics*. Edited by David Farrell Krell. New York: HarperCollins, 1991.

———. *Nietzsche, Volume IV: The Will to Power as Knowledge and as Metaphysics*. Edited by David Farrell Krell. New York: HarperCollins, 1991.

———. "Overcoming Metaphysics." In *The End of Philosophy*, translated by Joan Stambaugh, 84–110. Chicago: The University of Chicago Press, 2003.

———. *Pathmarks*. Edited by William McNeill. Cambridge: Cambridge University Press, 1998.

———. *The Phenomenology of Religious Life*. Translated by Matthias Fritsch and Jennifer Anna Gosetti-Ferencei. Bloomington and Indianapolis: Indiana University Press, 2004.

———. *The Principle of Reason*. Translated by Reginald Lilly. Bloomington: Indiana University Press, 1991.

———. "The Question Concerning Technology." In *The Question Concerning Technology and Other Essays*, translated by William Lovitt, 3–35. New York: Harper & Row, 1977.

———. "Science and Reflection." In *The Question Concerning Technology and Other Essays*, translated by William Lovitt, 155–182. New York: Harper & Row, 1977.

———. "Sketches for a History of Being as Metaphysics." In *The End of Philosophy*, translated by Joan Stambaugh, 55–74. Chicago: The University of Chicago Press, 1973.

———. "The Thing." In *Poetry, Language, Thought*, translated by Albert Hofstadter, 163–186. Harper & Row: New York, 1971.

———. *Towards the Definition of Philosophy*. Translated by Ted Sadler. New York and London: The Athlone Press, 2000.

———. "The Turning." In *The Question Concerning Technology and Other Essays*, translated by William Lovitt, 36–52. New York: Harper and Row, 1977.

———. "What Are Poets For?" In *Poetry, Language, Thought*, translated by Albert Hofstadter, 89–142. New York: Harper and Row, 1971.

———. *What Is a Thing?* Translated by W. B. Barton Jr. and Vera Deutsch. Chicago: Henry Regnery Company, 1967.

———. *What Is Called Thinking?* Translated by Fred D. Wieck and J. Glenn Gray. New York: Harper & Row, 1968.

———. "Why Do I Stay in the Provinces?" In *Heidegger: The Man and the Thinker*, edited by Thomas Sheehan, 27–30. Chicago: Precedent, 1981.

Heinberg, Richard. *Peak Everything: Waking Up to the Century of Declines*. Gabriola Island, BC, Canada: New Society, 2007.

Heinzerling, Lisa. "Climate Change, Human Health, and the Post-Cautionary Principle." *Georgetown Law Journal* 96, no. 4 (2008): 1–25.

Hsiao, Paul Shih-yi. "Heidegger and Our Translation of the *Tao Te Ching*." In *Heidegger and Asian Thought*, edited by Graham Parkes, 93–103. Honolulu: University of Hawaii Press, 1987.

———. *The Human and Environmental Impact of Fracking: How Fracturing Shale for Gas Affects Us and Our World*. Edited by Madelon Lubin Finkel. Santa Barbara, Denver, and Oxford: Prager, 2015.

Hume, David. *A Treatise of Human Nature*. Edited by David Fate Norton and Mary J. Norton. New York: Oxford University Press, 2000.

Husserl, Edmund. *Logical Investigations*, second edition. Translated and edited by Dermot Moran. London: Routledge, 2001.

Imort, Michael. " 'Eternal Forest—Eternal *Volk*': The Rhetoric and Reality of National Socialist Forest Policy." In *How Green Were the Nazis? Nature, Environment, and Nation in the Third Reich*, edited by Franz-Josef Brüggemeier, Mark Cioc, and Thomas Zeller, 171–203. Athens: Ohio University Press, 2005.

IPCC. "Summary for Policymakers." In *Climate Change 2014: Impacts, Adaptation, and Vulnerability. Part A: Global and Sectoral Aspects. Contribution of Working Group II to the Fifth Assessment Report of the Intergovernmental Panel on Climate Change*, edited by C. B. Field et al., 1–32. Cambridge and New York: Cambridge University Press, 2014.

Irwin, Ruth. *Heidegger, Politics and Climate Change: Risking It All*. New York: Continuum, 2008.

———. "Reflections on Modern Climate Change and Finitude." In *Climate Change and Philosophy: Transformational Possibilities*, edited by Ruth Irwin, 48–74. New York: Continuum, 2010.

Jamieson, Dale. "Ethics, Public Policy, and Global Warming." *Science, Technology, and Human Values* 17, no. 2 (1992): 139–153.

Jeffers, Robinson. *The Wild God of the World: An Anthology of Robinson Jeffers*. Edited by Albert Gelpi. Stanford: Stanford University Press, 2003.

Jung, Hwa Yol and Petee Jung. "To Save the Earth." *Philosophy Today* 19, no. 2 (1975): 108–117.

Kant, Immanuel. *Groundwork for the Metaphysics of Morals*. Edited and translated by Allen W. Wood. New Haven and London: Yale University Press, 2002.

Kennedy, Tara. "Book Review: *Heidegger and the Earth: Essays in Environmental Philosophy*." *Environmental Ethics* 33, no. 1 (2011): 93–96.

Khush, Gurdev S. "Genetically Modified Crops: The Fastest Adopted Crop Technology in the History of Modern Agriculture." *Agriculture and Food Security* 1, no. 14 (2012): 1–2.

Kolbert, Elizabeth. *The Sixth Extinction: An Unnatural History*. New York: Henry Holt and Company, 2014.

Kosugi, Takanobu. "Fail-Safe Solar Radiation Management Geoengineering." *Mitigation and Adaptation Strategies for Global Change* 18, no. 8 (2013): 1141–1166.

Krupp, Fred and Miriam Horn. *Earth: The Sequel: The Race to Reinvent Energy and Stop Global Warming*. New York: W.W. Norton & Company, 2009.

Kuhn, Thomas. *The Structure of Scientific Revolutions*. Chicago: University of Chicago Press, 1962.

Langer, Monika. "Nietzsche, Heidegger, and Merleau-Ponty: Some of Their Contributions and Limitations for 'Environmentalism.'" In *Eco-Phenomenology: Back to the Earth Itself*, edited by Charles S. Brown and Ted Toadvine, 103–120. Albany: State University of New York Press, 2003.

Lao Tsu. *Tao Te Ching*. Translated by Gia-Fu Feng and Jane English. New York: Vintage Books, 1972.

Lee, Kwang-sae. *East and West: Fusion of Horizons*. Paramus, N.J.: Homa & Sekey, 2006.

Leopold, Aldo. *A Sand County Almanac and Sketches Here and There*. Oxford: Oxford University Press, 1949.

Liddell, Henry George and Robert Scott. *An Intermediate Greek-English Lexicon*. Oxford: Oxford University Press, 2003.

Lynch, William T. "A Society of Baconians? The Collective Development of Bacon's Method in the Royal Society of London." In *Francis Bacon and the Refiguring of Early Modern Thought*, edited by Julie Robin Solomon and Catherine Gimelli Martin, 173–202. Hants, England and Burlington, Vt.: Ashgate, 2005.

Ma, Lin. *Heidegger on East-West Dialogue: Anticipating the Event*. New York and London: Routledge, 2008.

Marrone, Steven P. "Medieval Philosophy in Context." In *The Cambridge Companion to Medieval Philosophy*, edited by Arthur Stephen McGrade, 10–50. Cambridge: Cambridge University Press, 2003.

Marshall, Peter. *Nature's Web: Rethinking Our Place on Earth*. New York: Paragon House, 1993.

Maugeri, Leonardo. *The Age of Oil: The Mythology, History, and Future of the World's Most Controversial Resource*. Westport, Conn.: Praeger, 2006.

May, Reinhard. *Heidegger's Hidden Sources: East Asian Influences on His Work*, translated by Graham Parkes. New York: Routledge, 1996.

McDonagh, Sean. *The Greening of the Church*. London: G. Chapman Publishers, 1990.

McKibben, Bill. *Deep Economy: The Wealth of Communities and the Durable Future*. New York: St. Martin's, 2007.

———. *Eaarth: Making Life on a Tough New Planet*. New York: Henry Holt and Company, 2010.

McWhorter, Ladelle, ed. *Heidegger and the Earth: Essays in Environmental Philosophy*. Kirksville, Mo.: Thomas Jefferson University Press, 1992.

Moeller, Hans-Georg. *Daoism Explained: From the Dream of the Butterfly to the Fishnet Allegory.* Chicago and La Salle, Ill.: Open Court, 2004.

Mugula, Ben Belden. "The Need for Anthropocentric Approaches vis-à-vis Ecocentric Views in Conservation of Global Renewable Resources." *International Journal of Agricultural Sciences* 3, no. 2 (2013): 384–386.

Muir, John. *A Thousand-Mile Walk to the Gulf.* Edited by William Frederic Bade. Boston and New York: Houghton Mifflin, 1916.

Naess, Arne. *Ecology, Community and Lifestyle.* Translated and edited by David Rothenberg. Cambridge: Cambridge University Press, 1989.

———. *The Ecology of Wisdom: Writings by Arne Naess.* Edited by Alan Drengson and Bill Devall. Berkeley, Calif.: Counterpoint, 2008.

———. "The Shallow and the Deep, Long-Range Ecology Movement: A Summary." *Inquiry* 16, no. 1 (1973): 95–100.

Nelson, Eric Sean. "Heidegger and the Questionability of the Ethical." *Studia Phaenomenologica* 8, no. 1 (2008): 395–419.

———. "Responding to Heaven and Earth: Daoism, Heidegger and Ecology." *Environmental Philosophy* 1, no. 2 (2004): 65–74.

———. "Responding with Dao: Early Daoist Ethics and the Environment." *Philosophy East and West* 59, no. 3 (2009): 294–316.

Nietzsche, Friedrich. *Beyond Good and Evil: Prelude to a Philosophy of the Future.* Translated by Walter Kaufmann. New York: Vintage, 1989.

Nikiforuk, Andrew. *Tar Sands: Dirty Oil and the Future of a Continent*, revised and updated. Vancouver: D&M Publishers, 2010.

Olafson, Frederick A. *Heidegger and the Philosophy of Mind.* New Haven, Conn.: Yale University Press, 1987.

Oldroyd, David. *The Arch of Knowledge: An Introductory Study of the History of the Philosophy and Methodology of Science.* New York and London: Methuen, 1986.

———. "Only a God Can Save Us: *Der Spiegel*'s Interview with Martin Heidegger," translated by Maria P. Alter and John D. Caputo. *Philosophy Today* 20, no. 4 (1976): 267–284.

Palmer, Clare. "A Bibliographic Essay on Environmental Ethics." *Studies in Christian Ethics* 7, no. 1 (1994): 68–97.

Parkes, Graham. "Introduction." In *Heidegger and Asian Thought*, edited by Graham Parkes, 1–14. Honolulu: University of Hawaii Press, 1987.

———. "Lao-Zhuang and Heidegger on Nature and Technology." *Journal of Chinese Philosophy* 39, no. 4 (2012), 112–133.

———. "Preface." In Reinhard May, *Heidegger's Hidden Sources: East Asian Influences on His Work*, translated by Graham Parkes, v–xi. New York: Routledge, 1996.

Pence, Gregory E. *Designer Food: Mutant Harvest or Breadbasket of the World?* Lanham, Md.: Rowman & Littlefield, 2002.

Plato. *Republic.* Translated by G. M. A. Grube and C. D. C. Reeve. Indianapolis/Cambridge: Hackett Publishing Company, 1992.

Pöggeler, Otto. *The Paths of Heidegger's Life and Thought.* Translated by John Bailiff. Amherst, N.Y.: Prometheus, 1999.

Polt, Richard. *The Emergency of Being: On Heidegger's* Contributions to Philosophy. Ithaca and London: Cornell University Press, 2006.

———. *"Ereignis."* In *A Companion to Heidegger*, edited by Hubert L. Dreyfus and Mark Wrathall, 375–391. Malden, Mass.: Blackwell, 2005.

———. "A Heideggerian Critique of Cyberbeing." In *Horizons of Authenticity in Phenomenology, Existentialism, and Moral Psychology: Essays in Honor of Charles Guignon*, edited by Hans Pedersen and Megan Altman, 179–197. Dordrecht, Heidelberg, New York, and London: Springer, 2015.

Polt, Richard and Gregory Fried. "Introduction." In *Nature, History, State: 1933–1934*, translated by Richard Polt and Gregory Fried, 1–13. London and New York: Bloomsbury, 2013.

Principe, Lawrence M. *Scientific Revolution: A Very Short Introduction*. Oxford: Oxford University Press, 2011.

Regan, Tom. *The Case for Animal Rights*. Berkeley and Los Angeles: University of California Press, 2004.

Rentmeester, Casey. "A Kantian Look at Climate Change." *Essays in Philosophy* 11, no. 1 (2010): 76–86.

———. "Do No Harm: A Cross-Disciplinary, Cross-Cultural Climate Ethics." *De Ethica* 1, no. 2 (2014): 5–22.

Ricciardi, Anthony. "Are Modern Biological Invasions an Unprecedented Form of Global Change?" *Conservation Biology* 21, no. 2 (2007): 329–336.

Rockström, Johan et al. "A Safe Operating Space for Humanity." *Nature* 461, no. 7263 (2009): 472–475.

Rohrkrämer, Thomas. "Martin Heidegger, National Socialism, and Environmentalism." In *How Green Were the Nazis? Nature, Environment, and Nation in the Third Reich*, edited by Franz-Josef Brüggemeier, Mark Cioc, and Thomas Zeller, 171–203. Athens: Ohio University Press, 2005.

Schiermeier, Quirin. "Water: Purification with a Pinch of Salt." *Nature* 452, no. 7185 (2008): 260–261.

Schönfeld, Martin. "From Climate Ethics to Climate Philosophy." *Climate Philosophy Newsletter* 4, no. 1 (2010): 22–27.

———. "Ecosophy in the Climate Age." *Zhexue Wenhua* 39, no. 7 (2012): 69–90.

———. "How 'Real' Is Daoism? Triangulating Laozi, Kant, and Climate." *International Journal for Field-Being* 6, no. 1 (2007): 1–10.

Seidel, Georg. "Heidegger: Philosopher for Ecologists?" *Man and World* 4, no. 1 (1971): 93–99.

Sharr, Adam. *Heidegger's Hut*. Cambridge and London: The MIT Press, 2006.

Sheehan, Thomas. *Making Sense of Heidegger: A Paradigm Shift*. London and New York: Rowman & Littlefield, 2015.

———. "Nihilism: Heidegger/Jünger/Aristotle." In *Phenomenology: Japanese and American Perspectives*, edited by Burt C. Hopkins, 273–316. Boston: Kluwer Academic Publishers, 2010.

Singer, Peter. *Animal Liberation*. New York: HarperCollins, 2002.

———. "Famine, Affluence, and Morality." *Philosophy and Public Affairs* 1, no. 1 (1972): 229–243.

Skolimowski, Henryk. "The Dogma of Anti-Anthropocentrism and Ecophilosophy." *Environmental Ethics* 6, no. 3 (1984): 283–288.

Stambaugh, Joan. "The Future of Continental Philosophy." In *Writing the Politics of Difference*, edited by Hugh J. Silverman, 275–282. Albany: State University of New York Press, 1991.

———. "Heidegger, Taoism, and the Question of Metaphysics." In *Heidegger and Asian Thought*, edited by Graham Parkes, 79–92. Honolulu: University of Hawaii Press, 1987.

Staudenmaier, Peter. "Fascist Ideology: The 'Green Wing' of the Nazi Party and Its Historical Antecedents." In *Ecofascism: Lessons from the German Experience*, edited by Janet Biehl and Peter Staudenmaier, 5–31. Edinburgh and San Francisco: AK Press, 1995.

Taylor, Charles. "Heidegger, Language, and Ecology." In *Heidegger: A Critical Reader*, edited by Hubert L. Dreyfus and Harrison Hall, 247–269. Cambridge, Mass.: Blackwell, 1992.

Taylor, Paul W. *Respect for Nature: A Theory of Environmental Ethics*. Princeton, N.J.: Princeton University Press, 2011.

Thompson, Lonnie G. "Climate Change: The Evidence and Our Options." *The Behavior Analyst* 33, no. 2 (2010): 153–170.

Thomson, Iain. *Heidegger on Ontotheology: Technology and the Politics of Education*. Cambridge: Cambridge University Press, 2005.

———. "Ontology and Ethics at the Intersection of Phenomenology and Environmental Philosophy." *Inquiry* 47, no. 4 (2004): 380–412.

Thoreau, Henry David. *Walden.* Secaucus, N.J.: Longriver Press, 1976.

Thucydides. *The Peloponnesian War*. Translated by Steven Lattimore. Indianapolis: Hackett, 1998.

Vallega-Neu, Daniela. *Heidegger's* Contributions to Philosophy: *An Introduction*. Bloomington and Indianapolis: Indiana University Press, 2003.

Vaughan, Naomi E. and Timothy M. Lenton. "A Review of Climate Geoengineering Proposals." *Climatic Change* 109, no. 3 (2011): 758–761.

Wartenberg, Thomas E. "Heidegger." In *The Routledge Companion to Aesthetics*, second edition, edited by Berys Gaut and McIver Lopes, 147–158. New York: Routledge, 2001.

Webb, David. *Heidegger, Ethics, and the Practice of Ontology*. London and New York: Continuum, 2009.

White, Lynn, Jr. "The Historical Roots of Our Ecological Crisis." *Science* 155, no. 3767 (1967): 1203–1207.

Wohlfart, Guenter. "Heidegger and Laozi: *Wu* (Nothing)—On Chapter 11 of the *Daodejing*." *Journal of Chinese Philosophy* 30, no. 1 (2003): 39–59.

Young, Julian. *Heidegger's Later Philosophy*. Cambridge: Cambridge University Press, 2002.

Zimmerman, Michael E. *Contesting Earth's Future: Radical Ecology and Postmodernity*. Berkeley, Los Angeles, and London: University of California Press, 1994.

———. *Heidegger's Confrontation with Modernity: Technology, Politics, Art*. Bloomington and Indianapolis: Indiana University Press, 1990.

———. "Heidegger's Phenomenology and Contemporary Environmentalism." In *Eco-Phenomenology: Back to the Earth Itself*, edited by Charles S. Brown and Ted Toadvine, 73–102. Albany: State University of New York Press, 2003.

———. "Implications of Heidegger's Thought for Deep Ecology." *The Modern Schoolman* 64, no. 1 (1986): 19–43.

———. "Martin Heidegger: Anti-Naturalistic Critic of Technological Modernity." In *Minding Nature: The Philosophers of Ecology*, edited by David Macauley, 59–81. New York: Guilford, 1995.

———. "Rethinking the Heidegger-Deep Ecology Relationship." *Environmental Ethics* 15, no. 3 (1993): 195–224.

———. "Toward a Heideggerean *Ethos* for Radical Environmentalism." *Environmental Ethics* 5, no. 2 (1983): 99–131.

Index

About the Author

Casey Rentmeester is assistant professor of philosophy at Finlandia University. He has published various articles on continental philosophy, environmental philosophy, and Chinese philosophy and lives in Michigan's Upper Peninsula with his wife and daughter.